HERE TODAY, HERE TOMORROW

Transforming Your Workforce from
High-Turnover to **High-Retention**

Gregory P. Smith

Dearborn™
Trade Publishing
A **Kaplan Professional** Company

This publication is designed to provide accurate and authoritative information in regard to the subject matter covered. It is sold with the understanding that the publisher is not engaged in rendering legal, accounting, or other professional service. If legal advice or other expert assistance is required, the services of a competent professional person should be sought.

Senior Acquisitions Editor: Jean Iversen
Senior Managing Editor: Jack Kiburz
Interior and Cover Design: Design Solutions
Typesetting: Elizabeth Pitts

Library of Congress Cataloging-in-Publication Data

Smith, Gregory P. (Gregory Paul), 1953–
    Here today, here tomorrow : transforming your workforce from high-turnover to high-retention / Gregory P. Smith.
        p.   cm.
    Includes bibliographical references and index.
    ISBN 0-7931-4553-8 (paperback)
    1. Employee retention. 2. Job satisfaction.   I. Title.
    HF5549.5.R58 S63   2001
    658.3′14–dc21
                                                    2001002215

Dearborn Trade books are available at special quantity discounts to use for sales promotions, employee premiums, or educational purposes. Please call our Special Sales Department to order or for more information, at 800-621-9621, ext. 4410, or write Dearborn Trade Publishing, 155 N. Wacker Drive, Chicago, IL 60606-1719.

Advance Praise for *Here Today, Here Tomorrow*

"Realizing that the talent crisis isn't likely to go away anytime soon, smart companies are now taking extraordinary steps to ensure their best employees have reasons to stay and reasons to perform. In his latest book, Gregory P. Smith provides a comprehensive road map for not only attracting and keeping talented employees, but also for motivating them to achieve a higher level of performance. Chock full of practical ideas and real-world examples, *Here Today, Here Tomorrow* is a must-read for any leader who wants to create a high-retention business that achieves results. This book is unarguably a keeper."
David Shadovitz, Editor-in-Chief,
Human Resource Executive magazine

"Kudos for *Here Today, Here Tomorrow.* If you want to know the architectural key to building and retaining a stable, quality workforce, buy this book. Easy to read—easy to implement."
Dave Dibble, Director of Marketing, Sunshine Companies, Inc.

"Today's workforce brings many things to the table: creative thinking, new ideas, boundless energy, and some issues that have not been dealt with in the past. Continually, it is made apparent that employees are not willing to follow in the footsteps of prior generations. *Here Today, Here Tomorrow* is an outstanding tool for learning an approach that works across generations and ensures a successful future."
Donna J. Murphy, Senior Vice President, Jefferson Bank

"Gregory Smith's *Here Today, Here Tomorrow* provides the insight that today's leaders and managers need to hone their 'retentionship' skills. Filled with an intriguing combination of management theory, case studies, and practical tips, Mr. Smith reinforces what all successful leaders know: When it's all said and done, the ability to attract and retain high-quality talent is the basis of long-term success."
John Michael, President and COO, Ivan Allen Furniture Company (Atlanta, Georgia)

"This is a must-read for executives and business owners. No matter what size company you work in, the key to business success is attracting, keeping, and motivating your workforce. This book provides all those answers and more and will make a measurable difference on your bottom line and in your organization's future success."
Embree Robinson, President and CEO, TRC Staffing Services, Inc.

"Greg Smith has packed a ton of useful information into this little book. He makes a convincing case for retaining those employees we work so hard to recruit. No matter your organization, you can find dozens of useful ideas for treating people right and providing the benefits that matter to them. If this book had been available years ago, many leaders could have avoided much trial and error."
Carl Patton, President, Georgia State University

"Gregory Smith not only outlines many of the causes of turnover, but also gives you tried-and-true 'best of the best' practices you can adopt to improve retention. Most companies want to improve retention but don't know how. This book really helps with the how. All that's left is—just doing it!"
Tillman (TD) Hughes, Jr., Chief Executive Officer, La Rosa's Inc.

"In *Here Today, Here Tomorrow,* Greg Smith has crafted a comprehensive, practical, and very readable guide to help transform any organization into a high-retention workplace. As the demographics of the labor market change dramatically, employers must also change—to create work environments that attract, motivate, and retain talented people. Smith offers proven ways to help organizations in all sectors of the economy, public and private, meet this challenge."
Bob Lavigna, Senior Manager for Client Services, CPS Human Resource Services (former administrator, Merit Recruitment and Selection, State of Wisconsin)

*Dedicated to **Cathy, Heather, Hannah,** and **Garry,** and to the memory of my father-in-law, **Garry J. Still***

Contents

Chapter | 5

Flexible Benefits Build a More Loyal and Productive Workforce   71

Chapter | 6

Keep the Doorways and Pathways of Communication Open   97

Chapter | 7

Create a Charged Work Environment That Energizes and Engages   117

Chapter | 10

Help People Move Up or They Will Move Out   185

Chapter | **11**

Implementing the High-Retention Workplace   201

Acknowledgments

A s with most things in life, important accomplishments rarely come together based on one person's effort. The same is true with this book, which is the product of the collaborative efforts of many people. First and foremost I want to thank my wonderful wife, Cathy, who has supported me and been my silent partner for the past 24 years. Her insight, wisdom, and decisions have been the bedrock for a happy marriage, a strong family, and a successful business enterprise. During the many hours of writing and researching this book, she has tolerated my moodiness and irritability.

Special thanks to Betty Christian, who is a loyal friend and dedicated associate. Only a few people in this world are as supportive as Betty. She left retirement to work with me and has given more encouragement and confidence than anyone possible. She has helped with the development and editing of this book, and has promoted my company to thousands across the country.

I truly appreciate Jean Iversen Cook of Dearborn Trade Publishing, who provided me the opportunity to write this book. She is a true professional who exhibits patience and just the right amount of "moxie" to make things happen. The book would not have been possible without the keen insight and assistance of Anne Basye, an excellent writer and editor who took a less-than-complete manuscript and turned it into something intelligent and readable. Thanks to my literary agent, Jeff Herman, who expertly handled all the details.

The able team of Steve White, Richard DeMouy, Diane Jacobson, Pam Cook, and Roxanne Dzur of Choctaw Management Services Enterprise allowed me to practice what I preach. Also, special recognition goes to all the other staff members of this fine organization who make a valuable and important difference each day. To my friend Brian Howe, the president of Strategic Information for Teambuilding Inc., whose friendship and ideas I appreciate more than he realizes. Much appreciation to Sam Smiley of Rockdale Networks, who has kept all of our computers, networks, and data systems working during this book-writing process. Thanks to Susanne Houdek for her years of support and encouragement.

To all my friends and fellow alumni at North Georgia College and State University, where my first lessons on leadership began. Finally, many thanks and much appreciation to Linda Rudolph, Keith Senator, Nikkie Perry, Neal Banks, Crystal Pulliam, Tim Timmons, Linda Breeden, Candy Beam of Broadwell Printing, Dr. Timothy Park, Ted and Linda Bisterfield, Keith Herbert, Tom Turner, and all of my other friends, allies, and associates who made this book possible.

Introduction
The Labor Shortage Won't Go Away

When I started writing this book, employee retention was a sizzlingly hot topic. Unemployment was extraordinarily low, and the stock market was sky-high. Competition for qualified workers was so keen that managers practically came to blows over competent information technology, or IT, workers.

When I finished the book, layoffs were capturing the headlines. The dot-com meltdown was in full swing. Corporate giants like Lucent Technologies, GM, and Motorola were letting go thousands of people.

Despite these economic changes, the issue of employee retention is here to stay. The labor shortage that plagues employers at the height of an economic boom will not vanish. It may be temporarily off our radar now and then, but it will always be back, stronger than ever.

Regardless of the performance of the economy, we do not have enough quality people equipped with the right skills to fill all the jobs available—and it's going to get worse. The labor pool is drying up. No longer is there a bottomless pit of workers ready to knock on employers' doors. The growth rate of the workforce has been steadily declining since the 1970s. Both the U.S. Census Bureau and a report from the former Andersen Consulting indicate that the workforce will begin to experience a negative growth rate beginning in the year 2015.

Workers in the 25-to-44 age category—traditionally the source of executive talent—are already disappearing. Good frontline managers and supervisors are increasingly hard to find. Many information technology jobs are still in big demand. Vacancies in the food industry and health care field are driving human resources professionals to distraction.

In the long run, there will be more jobs than qualified workers. The tight job market of the late 1990s was just a taste of difficulties to come. The outlook—increasing competition for fewer qualified workers—will necessitate an enormous emphasis on the need to *retain* those workers.

Not many organizations are ready to meet this challenge.

Employers *say* they want loyal, motivated employees who will stay committed to their organization. But then they threaten these workers with layoffs and insult them with a work environment where people have to work longer hours to take up the slack of two or more people.

Our emphasis on short-term profits and shareholder return has shattered the concept of the "lifetime job." With that concept put out to pasture, today's workers know that their employers see them as expendable—so why should they give their best to an organization that may lay them off when profits go south?

Meanwhile, those very employers who see workers as expendable and not loyal tie up enormous amounts of time, money, and energy in recruiting and replacing an endless stream of workers. That's backward.

As our labor pool shrinks, employers must focus on creating a work environment that lets people work productively and effectively and makes them feel good enough to stay. That's the subject of this book.

Here Today, Here Tomorrow shows managers what it takes to create a positive work environment that attracts, keeps, and motivates its workforce to higher levels of performance. It is a complete guide to the key elements that can transform high-turnover industries to high-retention businesses.

Two key themes permeate this book. First, retention matters. A continual effort to replace departing workers—to keep the revolving door full, instead of stopping it altogether—is bleeding U.S. businesses dry. It's expensive to constantly replace people. The cost of attracting, recruiting, hiring, training, and getting new people up to speed is tremendously more costly as well as tremendously more wasteful than most realize.

Second, productivity is directly tied to retention. Companies with high turnover are at risk for low productivity. Studies from the Gallup organization show that employees who have an above-average attitude toward their work will generate 38 percent higher customer satisfaction scores, 22 percent higher productivity, and 27 percent higher profits for their companies.

The right work environment can achieve both of these goals. Whether a worker stays for 2 years or 20, he or she should be as productive as possible. If companies can't guarantee lifelong employment, at least they can create an environment that removes obstacles to productivity for the life of a job.

In this book, you'll read about companies with work environments that attract and retain people—and where people are willing to give their best. These environments aren't expensive. In fact, they save money. In many cases, they improve retention and productivity tremendously without lavish salaries or bonuses. And they certainly lower the expense of continually hiring and training new people.

This book shows why retention and productivity must become strategic issues of the highest priority. It introduces the elements of a high-retention workplace and shows how to implement them. It also offers vignettes and ideas from a wide range of organizations that have learned that a positive work environment creates happier, more productive workers and a healthier bottom line.

Why I Wrote This Book

I wrote this book for several reasons. The most compelling is the pain I feel when I see human potential going to waste. It's heartbreaking to see people who are so hamstrung by poor management or procedures that they are unable to enjoy what they do. Whether they quit outright or only mentally resign from achieving above-minimum performance, there are two losers—the individual and the business.

My viewpoint on human potential has been shaped by many years of working with the military. I joined the military for two main reasons: to follow in my father's footsteps and to learn how to become a leader. My early years in the military were very exciting, and I learned a great deal about leadership—the good and the bad.

But the higher I moved up the ranks, the more frustrated I became. Eventually, it seemed to me that what mattered wasn't ideas or initiative but rank, title, and the location of your office. In basic terms, bureaucracy replaced leadership. It was more important to protect the bureaucracy, the old way of doing things, than it was to improve.

Eventually, I found myself at the corporate level of the U.S. Army's medical headquarters in San Antonio, Texas. I was the director of quality management and strategic planning when the military was in the throes of change. The Berlin Wall had fallen and now the U.S. Army found itself without an enemy for the first time since the Cold War. Well, that's not entirely true. We did find another enemy: ourselves. We had become our own worst enemy.

During the 1980s and early 1990s, part of my job was to travel the nation to attend the best education and training sessions and look for innovative examples in the private sector. To my surprise, I found that many private sector businesses were just as bureaucratic as the military—sometimes more so.

Through the efforts of senior military leadership, we were able to help transform the military into a more flexible and more responsive entity. Those successes experienced by the military helped capture the attention of private sector businesses. When I left the military, I developed my own strategy, which combined the best ideas the military had to offer with the best ideas of the corporate side. With this knowledge I began working with other organizations interested in creating work environments that lead to higher retention and better productivity. Of all the lessons learned, the one that stands central is that retention, just like leadership, must begin at the top.

In this book, you'll meet dozens of CEOs who know that where they lead, their companies follow. When they decide to value their employees, to discard old mindsets and replace them with innovative new approaches, to replace ineffective management styles with flexible, effective management practices—it gets done. With the support of top management, companies can create environments that nurture employee retention and productivity.

In my travels and in working with my clients, I have found that every industry—from food to hardware to high-tech to tanning salons—wanted to know how to improve workforce retention and make employees more productive.

And in my travels, I found how. In researching this book, I talked with dozens of companies that have created humane, exciting, creative approaches to work—approaches that are energizing their people and increasing their profits.

The variations are exciting, but the recipe is simple:

- Select better managers and develop them into effective leaders.
- Hold managers responsible for retention in their departments.
- Focus on building relationships with people during their first week.
- Provide a productive work environment that limits work to 35 to 40 hours a week.
- Pay competitively and offer benefits that let employees take good care of themselves and their family members.
- Make people feel good about themselves and their work.
- Provide opportunities for learning and advancement.

Companies that practice these principles don't have to worry about losing employees. Their people feel provided for, and they are not going to jump ship for a $2-an-hour pay raise. It's a win–win situation. Workers enjoy their workplace and earn a decent salary, and employers save money they would otherwise invest in endless recruitment and training.

Meanwhile, you can bet that the same employers that have downsized their workforce will be recruiting their replacements very soon. Unfortunately, they will painfully discover how difficult it will be to find the same caliber of workforce they let go.

If you have smart, gifted, well-trained, and loyal workers who wouldn't leave your company for a million dollars, I congratulate you. If, on the other hand, you're ready to do what you can to bring the revolving door of personnel to a halt, read on. I hope this book will inspire you to take the actions necessary to make your business a place where your employees can say, *here today . . . and here tomorrow.*

Chapter | One

Here Today . . .
Gone Tomorrow!

The greatest tragedy in America is not the destruction of our natural resources, though that tragedy is great. The truly great tragedy is the destruction of our human resources by our failure to freely utilize our abilities, which means most men and women go to their graves with their music still in them. The tragedy is compounded when those of us in leadership positions do not utilize our abilities to properly direct and inspire those in our sphere of influence to become all they are capable of becoming.
(Oliver Wendell Holmes)

For Liecom Company, finding skilled workers was tough. After searching many months for a graphic designer, Liecom discovered Mary. Conscientious and hard working, Mary had recently graduated at the top of her class. She received offers from several other companies, but she liked what the recruiter told her about Liecom. The recruiter promised her a signing bonus, rapid acceleration, a teamwork environment, and great opportunities for personal and professional development. Mary accepted.

After two weeks on the job, Mary's opinion began to change. On several occasions, she was left behind to answer the phones while the rest of the department went out to lunch together. One morning, Barry, her supervisor, chewed her out in front of her coworkers. A few days later she was turned down for a training course because she was a "new employee."

Once bright and motivated, Mary began to develop a different attitude. At the end of the month Mary turned in her resignation, telling Barry she had gotten another job at higher pay somewhere else.

Why So Much Turnover?

It doesn't matter whether you run a pizza restaurant or a software development company. Finding qualified workers is hard. Every industry is having difficulty attracting, keeping, and motivating its workforce. What are the forces making it harder to hire and keep qualified people?

Fewer Workers, Better Times

Between 1992 and 2000, the powerful U.S. economy churned out jobs in everything from traditional brick-and-mortar businesses to Internet-based dot-com start-ups. More people were needed, but fewer were available to work. Plentiful jobs—reflected in an unemployment rate that dipped as low as 4 percent—gave no incentive for employees to stick with an inferior or demeaning work environment.

Turnover soared in every industry. In the food industry, turnover started at 87 percent and reached an unbelievable 117 percent annually among hourly workers. Registered nurses left their jobs, dissatisfied with their work environment. Nationwide turnover of nurses reached 18 percent, and in the South an incredible 40 percent. Even the tanning bed industry recently called me to help combat its high turnover rates.

Until the economy began to slow late in 2000, businesses in search of new help were doubling their recruiting and selection efforts and providing competitive training and development, compensation, and employee relations. They also ramped up employee benefits, increasing spending dramatically from $23.7 billion in 1960 to $266 billion in 1980 and to $747 billion in 1994, according to the Employee Benefits Research Institute. The cost of benefits continued to rise in the year 2000 with an overall 4.1 percent increase in wages and benefits by the end of December 2000. This was the largest increase since 1991 based on the need employers felt in order to attract and keep their workforce.

Some companies looked overseas for workers. Convenience chain 7-Eleven brought in 150 college-age workers from Eastern Europe, and Sea World in Orlando hired more than 70 international workers to fill seasonal positions. The low-wage food industry even considered robots as a way to meet its constant demand for new workers. Flipper, a robotic fast-food chef, turned out 9 hamburgers and 12 brown pancakes—all of uniform size—in just minutes in a demonstration at the National Restaurant Association convention. Built to handle the work of two employees in its 16-hour, 7-day-a-week shift, it even scraped the grease off the griddle—with no insurance, no taxes, no training, no holidays, and no absentee problems.

Competition for information technology (IT) workers (which reached new heights when 16 Internet service provider engineers and managers auctioned themselves on eBay for $3.14 million with an additional $320,000 signing bonus) forced employers to offer lavish salaries, generous stock options, and unusual perks to lure and keep qualified workers. Revenue Systems Incorporated (RSI), a software company in Atlanta, leased either a Z-3 or a 323 BMW to each of its 60 employees to keep until they quit. It's cheaper, RSI reasoned, to lease luxury cars than pay headhunters the same amount of money to replace their workers.

The economy began slowing and the stock market took a nosedive in the first quarter of 2001, but the labor supply continued to tighten. Census reports confirm that the growth rate of the workforce has been steadily declining since 1965. Already the growth rate is practically zero, and very soon, as Figures 1.1 and 1.2 show, it will be a negative number.

There are more jobs than people, period. Labor pools at all levels are reaching critical mass. When workers have options, there is little reason to stick with a bad organization.

Figure 1.1   Growth Rate of U.S. Labor Force

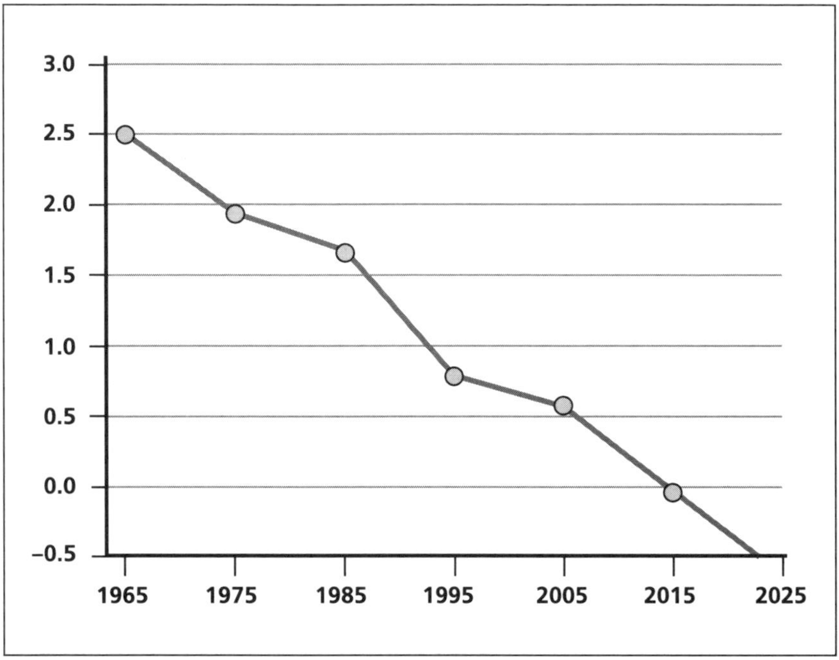

Source: U.S. Census Bureau and Department of Labor Statistics.

Higher Expectations

Most people today want more than just a "job"—that is, more than just an obligation with a decent paycheck attached to it. People are looking for more. They want meaning. Purpose. Younger workers especially want to align themselves with an organization or a cause that makes a difference.

But they also want money. Many college graduates entering the workforce expect to make $40,000 right off the bat and feel no compunction about trading up to another company and a better salary as soon as possible. During the 1990s, dot-coms and other high-tech firms fed these get-rich-quick dreams with generous stock options designed to lure high-priced talent. These high salary expectations have persuaded many people to jump ship.

Figure 1.2　Percentage Growth of Labor Force by Age Group

Age of Worker	% Change 1950–1960	% Change 1961–1970	% Change 1971–1980	% Change 1981–1990	% Change 2000–2005 (est)	% Change 2005–2010
16–19	41.7%	47.8%	–8.6%	–4.5%	10.6	6.1%
20–24	40.4	64.3	10.2	–9.0	7.9	4.8
25–34	1.0	57.5	43.3	0.4	–8.3	2.5
35–44	7.9	6.5	50.3	35.3	2.6	–6.6
45–54	20.4	6.7	6.2	43.0	27.1	8.5
55–64	21.8	10.2	3.2	4.1	24.9	21.5
65+	–2.3	–3.5	3.5	20.7	6.3	7.2

Source: U.S. Census Bureau, Department of Labor Statistics and Arthur Andersen.

High expectations for training and advancement have also caused many to grow dissatisfied with humdrum employers. Especially for information technology workers, constant training is a must, and they will abandon employers who do not help them keep up with continual changes in their field.

High expectations of flexibility are the final factor. Many people, struggling to stay in control of complicated lives and to seek a work/life balance, have shifted from traditional, full-time employment to a variety of flexible workforce options, including temporary and contract work, consulting, freelance work, and part-time and flextime work. In their search for flexibility, people will abandon rigid companies in favor of organizations that offer many ways to participate in their work environment.

Longer Hours, More Demanding Work

The average workweek grew from 43.6 hours in 1977 to 47.1 hours in 1997. One in five employees are required to work paid or unpaid overtime hours at least once a week with little notice. And 33 percent of all employees bring work home—a 10 percent increase since 1977. People have to work harder and faster just to keep up!

Workers have had enough. According to the *National Study of the Changing Workforce,* 64 percent of all employees want to work less. The workplace that insists on long hours and high demands is vulnerable. Low wages and long hours are simply not attractive to younger workers when they have more choices in an expanding economy! Much more attractive are workplaces that couple a decent living wage with nontraditional work options, such as flextime and working from home, or that limit work to 35 or 40 hours and no more.

Family Demands

Day care has been an issue for a couple of decades; now it's elder care. Twenty-five percent of the workforce has had to provide some type of elder care during the previous year. Employees who care for their parents spend up to 11 hours per week providing assistance. More than a third have to reduce their work hours to provide assistance. Men were just as likely as women to reduce their workweek to provide assistance to elders. Workers trying to balance complex family demands will migrate to the most supportive employer.

Changing Work Ethic

Many managers complain about the changing—some say disappearing—work ethic in America. Those who manage teenagers say it takes two people to get the work of one person. In the *Atlanta Journal-Constitution,* the manager of Zoo Atlanta complained that scheduling is useless: "They tell me when they want to work and when they don't. They show up when they want and leave when they want. No-shows are common. And it's not uncommon for a worker to clock out for lunch and not return. I feel powerless to do anything about it."

I've heard stories about people who have shown up for an interview and been hired but didn't show up for work the next day. Sometimes it seems that unreliability is epidemic. In addition, it's harder to find employees who have a strong work ethic and are willing to put in a "good day's work." Boardrooms across America complain about the mismatch of job skills and work ethics in the workforce. Some workers not only lack technical skills but have poor reading and writing skills, in addition to needing help in such basic work habits as showing up for work on time or calling in an absence.

A New Class of College Graduates

A new group of college graduates brings new challenges as well as new ideas into the labor market. Generation X and Generation Y employees want and demand such benefits as health care insurance, decent pay, and a clear separation between their work and their personal life. They tend to be less motivated by promises of overtime pay and more motivated by personal satisfaction with their job. The number one benefit for Generation X and Generation Y employees (Gen Xers and Gen Yers) is development and training. They want to grow in their jobs and learn new skills. Unlike their parents and grandparents, they do not anticipate staying with one job or company throughout their entire career. They expect to change jobs as they seek employment that offers them both better benefits and more opportunity for professional growth as well as personal fulfillment.

The Biggest Challenge: Meeting the Needs of an Increasingly Diverse Workforce

All of the factors listed above are important in analyzing the reasons behind high turnover. But in my view, the biggest impediment to a stable, loyal, productive workforce is a one-size-fits-all approach to management that fails to meet the needs of individual workers.

As traditional workers disappear, jobs are being filled by many different kinds of people: teenagers who have to balance work and educational responsibilities; working mothers who don't want to be away from their children full-time; older workers who are not ready for complete retirement but would be happy to cut back their hours; people eager to learn everything they can so they can start their own business; full-time workers; part-time workers; telecommuters; people who work at home or who live in one city and check into an office in another once or twice a month.

Over the past decade the workforce has also grown more diverse in cultures, generations, nationalities, and work arrangement needs. Each of these groups has different needs, attitudes, and expectations.

The Aging Workforce

Consider 45- to 65-year-old workers, who census figures show is the fastest-growing demographic. These older workers are willing to stay in the workforce longer or reenter it after early retirement. Many have reached financial independence and seek work with true purpose and meaning. According to Dr. Ira Wolfe, president of Success Performance Systems, by the year 2020 there will be 27.7 people aged 65 and older for every working-age adult—a 28.5 percent increase from 1980.

Yet most businesses continue to cater to rapidly diminishing younger workers. A survey conducted by the Society of Human Resource Managers shows that 65 percent of companies surveyed exerted no effort to recruit older workers for open positions. Eighty-one percent did not have benefit plans designed with older workers in mind.

Attitudes clash too. Whereas many older workers still believe "you're lucky to have a job," younger workers are developing a "free agent" mentality. Reared after the demise of the lifetime job, they believe it's not good to stay in one job for very long. Instead, they often seek to acquire as much experience and earn as much money as possible. Less willing to sell their

Figure 1.3 Four Generations in the Workplace

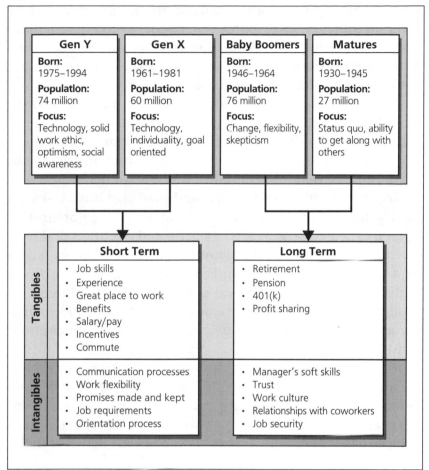

Gen Y	Gen X	Baby Boomers	Matures
Born: 1975–1994	**Born:** 1961–1981	**Born:** 1946–1964	**Born:** 1930–1945
Population: 74 million	**Population:** 60 million	**Population:** 76 million	**Population:** 27 million
Focus: Technology, solid work ethic, optimism, social awareness	**Focus:** Technology, individuality, goal oriented	**Focus:** Change, flexibility, skepticism	**Focus:** Status quo, ability to get along with others

	Short Term	Long Term
Tangibles	• Job skills • Experience • Great place to work • Benefits • Salary/pay • Incentives • Commute	• Retirement • Pension • 401(k) • Profit sharing
Intangibles	• Communication processes • Work flexibility • Promises made and kept • Job requirements • Orientation process	• Manager's soft skills • Trust • Work culture • Relationships with coworkers • Job security

soul to the organization and work 60 to 80 hours a week, they can be skeptical of institutions. Instead of living to work, they work to have a life. Conditioned by video games and the Internet for instant gratification, they are eager to seek greener pastures when a job grows dull or unrewarding.

Yet these two groups—actually four groups, as Figure 1.3 shows—work side by side. Today, 20-somethings even supervise people who were driving automobiles before they were born. "It weirds me out sometimes," says the 29-year-old president of the Web site builder Proteus.

Cultures also clash. Already the fastest-growing minority in the United States, Latinos will be the largest minority by 2005. In some city neighborhoods, residents come from more than 50 countries. This ethnic diversity isn't limited to corporations in cities. Many mid-sized and even small cities are home to large ethnic populations.

Diversity can go beyond culture, gender, and generation to include everything from communication and workstyles to physical ability, sexual orientation, educational background, and marital and parental status. Some human resources experts have even pointed to the "diversity of being."

In my consulting work, I've found that most businesses are totally unprepared for the challenges and opportunities offered by a diverse workforce. Hiring and retention practices are still aimed at older, more loyal workers. Benefit packages are rigid and offer too few options. Mentoring programs continue to assume that seasoned older workers should mentor younger people, when the reverse would promote understanding and appreciation for each generation's skills, ideas, and contributions.

In an ideal world, a company could create a unique employment package for every individual and offer the perfect combination of pay, benefits, and such intangibles as schedules and dress codes because it's hard to create a package that is as attractive to 22-year-olds as it is to 60-year-olds and everybody in between.

Today's array of employees places great demands on human resources and supervisors. Management skills need to be adapted to provide leadership to people who come in all sizes, colors, and styles—but would sometimes rather work with people just like themselves. Differences need to be managed sensitively, not ignored. Human resources departments need to create policies and programs that accommodate the changing work life needs of employees.

Money: Still a Factor?

Generous stock options and sky-high salaries still have their power to lure or keep employees. But even money doesn't affect everyone the same way. In his book *Money: Who Has How Much and Why,* Andrew Hacker, a professor of political science at Queens College in New York City, found that Gen Xers had the highest desire to become wealthy. Arlie Russel Hochschild, professor of sociology at the University of California at Berkeley and the codirector of the Center for Working Families, thinks Gen Xers have a more pessimistic view of life. Because they understand the impermanence of life, work, and marriages, they feel that the only thing left is money.

In his survey, Hacker discovered that men at all age levels (82 percent) are more interested in getting rich than women (68 percent). Asian Americans, Hispanics, and African Americans have a greater desire for money than whites, perhaps because they tend to be poorer than whites and provide more financial assistance to parents and in-laws. Asians have a stronger desire for wealth than any other cultural group and have the lowest level of consumer debt of all groups. People with undergraduate and graduate degrees were more likely to think money can buy freedom, including travel, starting a business, or financially supporting charities. But for all groups, the desire for riches declined as respondents grew older.

It's no surprise that money remains an important issue for working people—and a major, although not the most important, influence in a person's decision to stay in or leave a job. In general, however, money gets employees in the door, but it doesn't keep them there. Once employees' financial needs have been met, money's motivational influence diminishes, eclipsed by factors like recognition and advancement.

Reasons to Stay, Reasons to Go

If money isn't the main reason, then what causes people to stay with an organization and what causes them to go?

- A survey conducted by Robert Half International Inc. showed one-third of the executives now agree that the work environment is the most critical factor in keeping an employee satisfied in today's business world—an astonishing increase from only 9 percent in 1993.

- More than 40 percent of the respondents to a study by the public seminar company Linkage, Inc., said they would consider leaving their present employer for another job elsewhere for the same benefits if that job provided better career development and greater challenges.

- In its *National Study of the Changing Workforce,* the Families and Work Institute showed that earnings and benefits have only a 3 percent impact on "job satisfaction." "Job quality" and "workplace support" have a combined 70 percent impact—35 times greater than earnings and benefits!

My own *Workforce Retention Survey* reprinted in Appendix A confirmed my suspicions: *Although money is important, the work environment, the individual supervisor, and the quality of the job are the most important determinants in creating a productive work environment.* We have to pay people well, but it is impossible to pay them to be happy and productive; something else is needed.

Even though 55 percent of the respondents in my survey answered "salary" when asked, What are the reasons you stay at your present job? other responses included "challenging job assignments," "interesting work," "benefits," "flexibility in work hours," and "good boss." Thirty-nine percent said they wanted to feel they had "a purpose" on the job. Varied work assignments and career opportunities were also important.

Money became even less important when people were asked, "What causes you the greatest dissatisfaction at work?" "Lack of appreciation" led the list, followed by "too much paperwork" and "problems with supervisors." Only 20 percent of the respondents identified "pay and benefits" as a source of dissatisfaction, but 20 percent also identified "lack of training and development" and "lack of opportunity." It appears that what keeps people at an organization is different from what keeps them *satisfied* at an organization.

From my years of experience as a consultant, I've identified a Top Ten list of reasons why people leave jobs:

1. Management demands that one person do the jobs of two or more people, resulting in longer days and weekend work.
2. Management cuts back on administrative help, forcing professional workers to use their time copying, stapling, collating, filing, and doing other clerical duties.
3. Management puts a freeze on raises and promotions when an employee can easily find a job paying 20 to 30 percent more somewhere else.
4. Management doesn't allow the rank and file to make decisions or allow them pride of ownership. A visitor to my Web site e-mailed me a message that said, "Forget about the 'professional' decisions—how about when you can't even select the company's holiday card without the president rejecting it for one of his own taste?"
5. Management constantly reorganizes, shuffles people around, and changes direction constantly.
6. Management doesn't have or take the time to clarify goals and decisions. Therefore, it rejects work after it was completed, damaging the morale and esteem of those who prepared it.
7. Management shows favoritism and gives some workers better offices, trips to conferences, and the like.

8. Management relocates the offices to another location, forcing employees to quit or double their commute.

9. Management promotes someone who lacks training and/or necessary experience to supervisor, alienating staff and driving away good employees.

10. Management creates a rigid structure and then allows departments to compete against each other while at the same time preaching teamwork and cooperation.

Interesting, isn't it, that all ten factors begin with the phrase "Management . . . ."?

Interesting, too, is just how many of these high-turnover factors are preventable. My retention survey confirmed the truth of the saying, "Employees don't quit their companies, they quit their bosses." Thirty-five percent of the respondents answered yes to the question, "Was the attitude of your direct supervisor/manager the primary factor in your quitting a previous job?"

I believe soft management skills—people skills—are the critical element in battling high turnover and creating a culture of retentionship. My Workforce Retention Survey shows that management needs to communicate better, be more appreciative, show more genuine concern, and so on. But if I asked management about the answers to my survey, some would undoubtedly sneer that their workers are "a bunch of whiners always wanting stuff!"

This standoff is a result of the traditional management model, which creates a "we/they" mindset. "It's us against the management," workers might declare. "It's us against our employees," management might reply. This crippling "we/they" perspective goes nowhere, and it needs to be replaced by a new culture of retention, which I examine in Chapter 2.

Bad Management Driving Good Employees Away

The manager of this restaurant is a real piece of work. He is 27 and is more interested in paying attention to one of the 16-year-old girls here than the business that he is supposed to be growing.

We also have driver problems. People who come in and quit without giving two weeks' notice and people who are late or don't care to do anything above the call of duty or any extra work. People who won't close at night or take deliveries downtown, even though they would get an extra $2 to $3 per downtown delivery.

When we hire new people, they don't stay long because they think the work is too hard or the pay is not enough, even though the owner pays above the minimum wage if you prove yourself. The problem is no one wants to stick around and prove themselves because they can go somewhere else and immediately make seven bucks an hour to start. No one wants to put in their dues anymore.

The owner and I put up with this crap because we need bodies in the place to do the work. We have a few shining stars, but they are the minority. There is no formal training program, sexual harassment stipulations, rules, or regulations. People work there because they can put their time in and go home. Nobody really cares about being a customer support type of employee.

The few of us who do care end up doing most of the work and it's getting really frustrating. The owner is at the age where he is ready to give up but still needs the income. He cannot compete against the chain restaurants. He has only two stores, and the lady who partners one has stopped paying her commissions. Everybody is walking all over this guy and it's starting to hurt the business and the product output. The sad part is that he has a really good product line and has had for 33 years. I hate to see this get ruined.

The restaurant itself needs some care—new carpeting, paint, flooring, lights in the back lot, and the like. If things keep up like this and we can't find valuable employees, the business will certainly continue to drop and eventually die. What can we do to get and keep good employees? (Retentionship Seminar attendee)

Needed: A New Workplace Paradigm

Let's get back to the story of Mary, who left Liecom after only a month of employment. What went wrong?

Basically, Liecom didn't keep its promises, and Barry, through his own negligence, chased Mary out the door.

The recruiter promised Mary advancement, educational opportunities, and more. But instead of delivering on the promises, Barry operated under the old paradigm—the one that insists employees must earn their stripes before they collect opportunities. From Barry's point of view, manning the phones while everyone else eats is simply part of paying dues. Training is a perk that only comes once you've paid them.

Barry suffers from an awareness problem. He doesn't understand that employees have psychological as well as financial needs and that in today's economy those psychological needs are the key to retaining productive people.

What could Barry have done differently?

On her first day, Mary should have been given a "buddy" to introduce her to Liecom and be a resource for Mary's questions. She should have been included in lunches and encouraged to join the training class as soon as possible. Barry should have set aside time for a frank conversation to find out what Mary expected from her new job and then try to meet those expectations.

Instead, Barry reinforced the old hierarchy. Rather than including Mary in training and development programs, he wanted her to earn her stripes the same way he did. Maybe he thought that giving opportunities to a new employee is tantamount to letting her get something for nothing.

He was wrong.

The old hierarchy that Barry enforced is a barrier to productivity. As a consultant, I tell managers to forget ranking and hierarchy and get to work helping people reach their potential and understand what they expect. Forget the hierarchical model and its emphasis on seniority and longevity. New hires aren't dummies. Even CEOs and company presidents need to be able to reach out to the most junior person and find out what he or she needs and expects.

A new paradigm is afoot, especially among younger workers. High achievers with excellent skills need to be treated differently. They need to be provided the same opportunities and in some cases even more opportunities than their elders.

Everyone, regardless of age, gender, culture, or employment status, needs to be treated with respect and dignity. People who are ignored or treated disrespectfully may show up for work but do very little. I can punch a keyboard for eight hours, or I can look for new challenges, seek out problems to solve, and be more productive. It depends on my attitude. It's up to management to create an environment that nurtures a positive, productive attitude.

Finally, everyone needs to be treated as an individual. Each new employee brings a totally new set of expectations, needs, and problems. Balancing these needs and expectations takes more time and management skill than ever before.

Unfortunately, as the ranks of managers thin, the wrong people are often promoted to management—people with limited vision for the workplace and no soft skills at all! Bad management promotes high turnover. But if you select managers with care and show them how to create a positive, productive work environment, people will stay longer and perform better.

The Changes Are Permanent

In my work as a management consultant, I get to take a privileged view inside many companies. Believe me, I've seen winners, and I've seen losers.

The winners are adapting to the new paradigm of work. The losers are sticking to the old paradigm. Because their management is not adapting to permanent changes in the workforce, they *will* be history tomorrow.

Good intentions don't count. Good intentions will not make your company a winner. It's time to wake up and acknowledge that traditional management methods are no longer effective. What worked yesterday no longer works today and will get us in trouble. Whether the economy is strong or weak, it's time to change direction and begin to create environments where employees can be as productive and dedicated as possible.

Prescription | for Action

- Treat people as individuals and not as groups.
- Eliminate the slogan, "We've always done it that way."
- Realize diversity is not limited merely to race and gender but includes all cultural backgrounds, physical ability, work styles, parental status, and the different age groups.
- Make diversity a strength for the entire organization.
- Encourage managers to create an environment that includes differences in people and values.
- Let the younger workforce mentor the older workforce and vice versa.
- Ensure that younger workers take active roles in planning and coordinating activities.
- Train managers and supervisors about their role in managing a diverse workforce.
- Create special observances and special emphasis days to help educate the workforce about the contributions of diverse groups.
- Work to eliminate stereotypes that cause mental barriers to full employment.
- Ensure that people chosen for training, conferences, and special projects fairly represent the workforce as a whole.
- Ensure that all people are fairly considered for promotions and pay raises.
- Identify the retention factors for each type of employee category.

Chapter Two

Retentionship: A New Strategy Based on Action

The antidote to high turnover is *retentionship*—the process of attracting, selecting, caring about, training, developing, and keeping a workforce so that it can perform its jobs in an organization.

Retentionship has as its ultimate goal creating a work environment that allows good employees to stay as long as possible, allows mismatched employees to leave sooner or find more compatible jobs elsewhere, and allows employees to become more productive.

Every organization needs to practice retentionship. Although some employees may be more vulnerable than others— a good IT engineer may get three to four job offers each week— every employee contributes to the bottom line. Even a customer service person in a laundromat or a server in a restaurant is a key employee, especially if she makes each customer's experience as pleasant and productive as possible. Her departure would definitely have an impact on her customers and the success of the business. So while you might want to invest many more dollars in retentionship strategies for high-priced, high-profile, hard-to-replace executives, it is important to spend time and money on everyone. In a tight job market, recruiters and other employers feel no shame about shopping for good people inside your organization. If someone offers a service that another company wants, he or she is vulnerable.

No matter what kind of job your people have, someone is trying to steal them away. Don't blindly believe that your employees are happy and content just because you are. Accept the fact that 30 to 50 percent of your workforce is considering leaving your job for another. They may be perfectly happy with their job and still think about leaving. Thirty percent of the respondents in my survey answered yes to the question, "Are you presently considering leaving your job for another?" Another 6 percent answered maybe.

A Great Return on Investment

The first and foremost reason to practice retentionship is cost. Even a small effort can save plenty of money. Studies show that at a minimum, it costs $4,000 to $7,000 to replace an hourly low-wage employee and up to $40,000 to replace a midlevel, salaried employee. One Silicon Valley company I know estimates that the cost of replacing the average employee is $125,000. The Saratoga Institute and Hewitt Associates estimate that the productivity cost of replacing employees can cost between one to two and a half times the salary of the job opening. Figure 2.1 lists the factors to consider when estimating the cost of replacing a worker. Figure 2.2 calculates the cost of replacing someone who earns $48,000 a year. The annual impact of multiple departures can be staggering, as Figure 2.3 shows.

The most effective retentionship strategy is prevention. Recruiting and replacing your workforce is much more expensive. Spending most of your time on recruiting is similar to allowing your house to burn down instead of purchasing a smoke detector—or having your lung removed instead of quitting smoking. Prevention is always less expensive and wiser, especially when it comes to replacing top performers.

All employees are important, but they are only equal in the eyes of God, says Dr. John Sullivan, professor of human resources at San Francisco State University. In the realm of economics, Sullivan believes, some performers are worth more

Figure 2.1   Replacement and Turnover Costs

The costs associated with replacement and turnover vary according to the salary level and job responsibilities of the employee. To come up with an approximate cost estimate, consider the following factors:

Departure Costs
- Downtime—Counterproductive time and leaves of absence taken by the departing employee
- Administrative—Time taken by administrative personnel in terminating such items as benefits and insurance, communications, and related paperwork
- Exit interviews—Time associated with interviewing an employee prior to departure

Replacement Costs
- Advertising—Costs associated with designing, writing, and placing ads in newspapers, Web sites, and the like
- Screening—Time it takes to screen résumés.
- Interviewing—Time involved in calling, scheduling, and conducting interviews with applicants
- Hiring—Administration of tests, background investigations, reference checking, taking physical exams, and making offers and counteroffers
- Administration—Time required for setting up benefit packages, 401(k) plans, and Social Security and for completing forms and entering data into computer system
- Orientation—Depending on the level of responsibility, time range of one day to two weeks

Training and Development Costs
- Training costs—Costs to bring a person to a satisfactory level of competency that vary depending on the level of responsibility
- Coaching—Costs of on-the-job development to further improve job performance
- Equipment costs—Costs of new items of equipment, such as safety shoes, glasses, computer equipment, uniforms, cell phones, identity badges, and the like, depending on jobs of new employees

Miscellaneous Costs
These are difficult to measure but are additional costs associated with replacement and turnover.
- Overtime pay
- Lost opportunities
- Lost business
- Damaged goodwill
- Departure of friends/coworkers
- Damaged morale

Figure 2.2   Cost of Replacing a $48,000 Employee

Departure Costs Downtime, administrative services, and exit interviews	$ 3,000
Replacement Costs Advertising, screening, interviewing, hiring, checking, administration, and orientation of new employee	$ 8,000
Training and Development Costs Training of new employee, coaching, and equipment costs	$ 7,000
Miscellaneous Costs Overtime pay, lost opportunities, lost business, damaged goodwill, departure of friends/coworkers, damaged morale, and poor service to customers	$22,000
Total Cost	$40,000

than others. Consider Michael Jordan and the Chicago Bulls. Was Jordan equal to his teammates? Michael Jordan would have stayed with the Bulls and not retired if Phil Jackson had stayed on as coach. How are the Chicago Bulls doing now? Was the decision to let Michael Jordan retire worth it?

Consider the economic cost of replacing these key individuals:

- Operating room nurse–$80 thousand
- Average engineer in Silicon Valley–$200 thousand
- Top microchip product development team leader–$29 million
- Airline pilot who makes a mistake–??

Why Doesn't Everybody Practice Retention?

In spite of the staggering cost of turnover, Development Dimensions International reports that 54 percent of businesses do not have a formal retentionship program. In my survey, 61 percent of the respondents gave their organizations a failing grade on the question, "How would you rate the efforts of your company to retain good people?"

Figure 2.3   Productivity Costs of Turnover in XYZ Company

200 Employees ×	15% Annual Turnover	= 30 Employees
Average annual salary is $40,000	Monthly salary is $3,333 × 30 Employees	= $99,990
Average lost time per employee is one month	× 30 Employees	= 30 Months
30 × $99,990 = $2,999,700	$2,999,700 × 2 (replacement cost)	= $5,999,400 per year

Why don't these organizations have retentionship programs?

- Blind acceptance that certain jobs have high turnover
- Failure to accept responsibility for retaining good people
- Responsibility for retention seen as human resources department's alone—not management's
- Belief that a counteroffer can prevent losing a good employee
- Unawareness of how much turnover really reduces the bottom line
- Feeling that it takes too much time
- Absence of a management accountability system

Reasons to have a retentionship program:

- Improves company reputation
- Reduces turnover of critical employees
- Keeps competitors from stealing your workers
- Promotes positive word-of-mouth from employees
- Increases productivity
- Reduces costs and time spent replacing workers
- Simplifies time and effort for managers
- Ensures knowledge stays with the company
- Good companies attract good people

- Removes the stigma of employees returning to their former organization if new job doesn't work out

The Retentionship Process

To find out whether you need a retentionship process, write yes or no on a separate sheet of paper for each of these seven statements:

1. I identify the jobs in my organization that have the highest turnover and investigate why.
2. I conduct postexit interviews 30 to 90 days after an employee leaves the organization to find out the real reason the employee left.
3. I hold my managers accountable for turnover in their department.
4. I reward my managers for high retention in their department.
5. A part of every meeting is dedicated to staff retention and morale.
6. We have a good orientation program for new employees.
7. We go out of our way to communicate with our employees.

If you get more than two no's, you need to get serious about retentionship.

Retention Means Productivity

Costs alone won't persuade you to invest in a retention strategy. Consider the issue of *productivity.*

Productivity and retention go hand in hand. Improve one, and you improve the other. Why? Many traditional, hierarchically based organizations restrict the free exchange of ideas and discourage individual initiative and motivation. After all, ideas and initiative create change, and many systems simply don't want to. They protect themselves with a complex bureaucracy and unwieldy procedures that become obstacles to productivity. Workers become slaves of the system and end up feeling blocked, unchallenged, and little more than robots waiting for the next command.

Constant reorganizations, a stultifying routine, coworkers with bad attitudes, micromanagement, suspicious management, no authority to fix errors or implement ideas, people who play the "who can stay latest" game—all of these are impediments to productivity as well as an incentive to leave. No one really wants to work—or can—in this kind of environment!

Retention means nothing if workers merely take up space. In a survey conducted by the Public Agenda Foundation in New York, 50 percent of the respondents said they fail to put effort into their job over and beyond what is required. Three out of four people said they had the capability of becoming more effective than they were.

In a high-retention work environment, employees *can* become more effective. If you pay people well and provide good leadership—create a sense of belonging and purpose and eliminate the frustration of constant reorganization that drives people out the door—then it's possible to transform average or even poor performers into highly productive people.

In fact, even though top performers are important, I think it's a bad idea to focus exclusively on them. Books and articles on "Keeping Your Best Performers" and "Attracting and Keeping Your Top Talent" offend me. A students may be top performers in school, but getting As doesn't necessarily mean these students are going to be successful, hold a job, and make good decisions.

If you invest in programs that improve the work environment and raise the performance bar, you can help everyone become a top performer. And performance is a prerequisite for building a productive, competitive organization. Together, performance and productivity are the gold standard of today's business climate. If your company is not productive, it will be overwhelmed and perhaps eliminated by a younger, more ath-

letic company whose work environment does promote productivity and performance for all.

Leadership Makes the Difference

Leadership is the most critical factor in determining whether
a company invests in creating a high-retention culture.

I called my company Chart Your Course because I believe
businesses, like sailing ships, need a captain to keep them on
course. It's up to the captain to keep his or her eye on the destination and direct the crew to carefully trim the sails for maximum performance, speed, and direction.

Leaders are more than just figureheads. In carrying out
their responsibility of setting the direction, speed, and performance of the individuals within a company, they are ever
present: touching, motivating, talking, checking, removing,
training, preparing, breathing, active, moving about, and creating change. Responsibility for setting direction can't be del-
egated or left to a computer. Businesses that have replaced
their leaders with technicians, their brains with a hard drive,
are in for a rude surprise.

Leadership is responsible for everything the organization
does or fails to do. It's up to leaders to scan the horizon for
challenges, obstacles, and catalysts for change. They also need
to look below the surface for problems within the ship. Leadership needs to listen to the crew below deck, for they usually
have the best ideas and solutions.

It's also up to leaders to keep an organization from becoming rigid, inflexible, and difficult to steer toward change.
Course changes happen quickly. Leaders need to encourage
the kind of communication that lets information flow freely to
everyone on all decks, so that everyone knows what to do if a
sudden correction in course is required.

My nautical theme may sound old-fashioned, but it's very
pertinent today. A strong, effective leader is a prerequisite for
a successful retention program. In fact, it can't be created with-

out one. When the captain is invested in retentionship, the crew will follow suit.

The Eight Elements of the High-Retention Organization

There are many ways to create a high-retention culture. In my years as a consultant, I have identified eight basic elements that are essential to the high-retention organization. Each one, like the sails of a ship, can harness the power of the wind, but all eight are needed to transform an organization. A sail that is not properly set or is missing hinders the ship and causes frustration among the crew.

Each of the eight elements introduced here is discussed at length in its own chapter, which offers examples of companies benefiting from each element and provides ideas you can use to infuse the element into your organization. Chapter 11 explains how to implement a formal retentionship program that brings all eight elements together.

1. A clear sense of direction and purpose.   People want to be part of an organization that stands for something and gives them personal fulfillment and meaning. When an organization means something, people are willing to give more. That's why people work for nonprofit organizations or spend their off-work hours leading Scout troops and building houses for Habitat for Humanity.

Chapter 3 shows how employers can create meaning and purpose in their organization, align employees with its mission, and nurture a more dedicated, productive, and profitable crew.

2. Caring management.   Interpersonal skills are an essential element of the high-retention culture. People want to feel that management cares and is concerned for them as individuals, yet poor soft skills are one of the biggest factors that drive people away. Chapter 4 shows leaders how to create an environment that values relationships and people.

3. Flexible benefits and schedules adapted to the needs of the individual.   In today's workplace, flexibility rules. One-size-fits-all approaches to benefits have long since lost their effectiveness. Workers will migrate to companies whose benefit packages and schedules help them meet the demands of their life, whether they are single parents, adults who care for aging parents, older workers, younger workers, part-time workers, or telecommuters. Chapter 5 is replete with innovative benefit programs that have proven effective for high-retention companies.

4. Open communication.   In our technological age, people have a large appetite for information, and they want it instantly. High-retention workplaces place a high priority on delivering the right information to the right people at the right time using the right methodology. Companies that leave employees in the dark risk damaging morale and motivation—not to mention compromising their ability to make a quick change in course in the marketplace. Chapter 6 explains how to create a "high-access" culture that facilitates change.

5. A charged work environment.   People want to enjoy their work. They shun boring, bureaucratic, lifeless work environments. That's why high-retention workplaces don't bother with traditional ways of doing things. They find new ways to make work mentally engaging and physically energizing. They also ask for, listen to, and implement the ideas and suggestions of those who work for them. Chapter 7 shows how to create a charged work environment that will increase retention and productivity while lowering turnover.

6. Performance management.   It is becoming increasingly more difficult finding competent, motivated workers who have good attitudes and work ethics. Because of this, knowing how to manage performance is much more important in creating a high-retention workplace. Performance management includes a series of tools, techniques, and processes that can help align an individual and his or her behavior with the goals of the business enterprise. Chapter 8 introduces the "ABC" model and shows how to emphasize actions that stimulate the right behaviors and reinforce those behaviors with consequences for productive work habits and ethics.

7. Reward and recognition.   All humans need to feel appreciated. Reward and recognition programs help meet that need. Chapter 9 shows why a positive workplace that rewards and recognizes people builds higher productivity and loyalty and can engender behavior that leads to organizational success.

8. Training and development.   Today's workers want opportunity. They want to develop their skills and potential and enhance their ability to contribute and succeed. Chapter 10 shows how training and development give people greater control and ownership over their job, making them more capable of taking care of customers and creating better management-employee relationships.

SAS Institute: A Calm Ship in a Sea of Turbulence

An example of an organization that provides a holistic work environment is SAS Institute Inc., located in North Carolina's Research Triangle Park.

SAS resembles a college campus more than a software development company. Everything from the baby grand piano in the company cafeteria to the giant outdoor chess board indicates that this is a world apart. *Fortune* magazine lists it as one of the Top 100 Best Places to Work, and employees agree. Turnover hovers around 3.7 percent and has never exceeded 5 percent in its 20 years of existence. The national average for most industries is 15 to 20 percent. Many employees have loyalty stronger than any glue made. One graphic designer routinely turns down job offers from Silicon Valley for as much as 40 percent more money.

Many people say working at SAS is like working with your family. Its 5,400 employees find a nurturing environment that in some cases is the closest thing to a real family that many people have experienced. The benefits and perks go beyond what most businesses are willing to do for their employees, including these:

- Unlimited sick leave: There is no limit on how much sick leave employees can use. Bob Goodnight, SAS president, Ph.D., and billionaire, believes if you treat adults like adults, they will act as adults. It's no problem whether you are out sick for six days or six months.

- Onsite day care: For $250 a month, employees can place their children in the day care facility. Parents are encouraged to eat lunch and dinner with their children. The company cafeteria is equipped with high chairs.

- Free family health care: In lieu of health insurance, SAS staffs a medical clinic 24 hours a day for employees and their family members. This saves the company $300,000 a year in health insurance costs.

- Equal pay for equal work: Many businesses disaffect good employees by starting new hires at higher salaries than those of old employees. Not at SAS. If SAS has to hire new employees and pay them more, all employees with the same skill levels receive the same pay raise. The average salary is $50,000 a year.

- Thirty-five-hour workweeks: All employees work five seven-hour workdays. All operations close at 5 PM.

- Break areas and free food: Each floor has its own break area stocked with complimentary refreshments, including all the M&Ms employees can eat. SAS spends $45,000 annually on 22 tons of the little chocolate candies.

Loyalty can't be bought by benefits and perks, but SAS appears to have created a workplace where employees know they are cared for, trusted, and treated like adults.

Prescription | for Action

- Make sure the human resources department makes efforts to increase productivity and takes a proactive role in retention.
- Start measuring the cost of turnover and make it part of a meeting discussion.
- Focus energy on the key jobs that have the most impact on profitability.
- Human resources personnel must understand which departments, jobs, and products/services have the greatest impact on profitability.
- Make managers aware of the unique differences and expectations of the workforce.
- The human resources department must be involved in strategic planning.
- Constantly look for new ways of improving existing products/services.

Chapter Three

Provide a Clear Sense of Direction and Purpose

O ne core truth supersedes all backgrounds, cultures, and generations: people want to be part of an organization that means something.

When an organization means something, people are willing to give more. Let's face it: most employees have a "here today, gone tomorrow" attitude toward their work. They know their jobs may vanish when the company hits hard times or changes direction. With this kind of skeptical attitude, their loyalty to their employer may be only skin-deep.

But when meaning is present, loyalty is deeper. That's why people work for nonprofit organizations or dedicate themselves to building houses for Habitat for Humanity. And it's the reason why an employer that can create meaning and purpose—and align its employees with its mission—will have a more dedicated, productive, and profitable crew.

The Three Directions of Leadership

When meaning is present, people will give their allegiance to an organization. When it's not present, they simply won't. Soldiers are a good example. Even in combat, they don't blindly follow orders when their life is in harm's way. They first must believe in the purpose and the direction in which they are being led. In the midst of battle, they look at their leader and think, "Is this person going to lead me or get me killed?"

A job title doesn't make a person a leader. *Leader* is a title only others can bestow. Leaders must travel the gauntlet with those they lead *before* they are accepted as the leader. Until leaders prove themselves, they cannot gain the respect and trust of those they are in charge of.

The movie *Saving Private Ryan* illustrated this principle in its portrayal of the relationship between the soldiers, the mission, and the captain, who provided the glue that held the unit together. In the movie it's possible to see three important shifts or transitions in Captain Miller's leadership style. I call these three shifts the "Directions of Leadership."

The lowest level or form of leadership is *direction by fear.* On Omaha Beach, orders were direct and to the point. Life or death—do what you are told because there is no time to think. Leaders have to think, push themselves forward, and give orders for the group. What is good for the group must outweigh what is good for the individual.

The second level of leadership is *direction by respect.* Captain Miller had a charismatic effect on his men based on trust and respect. He revealed only enough about himself to maintain professional objectivity, keeping secret his career before the war. He couldn't afford to do anything that would compromise the mission. The men's respect—and their curiosity—were so great that Miller's troops even started a cash lottery for the person who could guess what the captain did for a living as a civilian.

Direction by fear and direction by respect can go only so far. The highest level of leadership is *direction by purpose.* Captain Miller's transition to this level is depicted in a scene on the hill of the enemy radar station. During the platoon's progress into enemy territory, doubts about Captain Miller's leadership and the mission had been surfacing. Feelings and emotions had worn thin as the men wondered why one man is worth risking eight lives. Now, upset with his decision to charge the hill that resulted in the death of their buddy, the group is about to mutiny against Captain Miller. Pistol in hand, the first sergeant is ready to shoot one of his own men. As he threatens to pull the trigger, Captain Miller breaks the tension. He tells them the secret: what he did before the war. "I was a schoolteacher," he said. In the silence that followed, you could feel the pressure evaporate and the soldiers thinking, "Damn, if he is a schoolteacher, what am I complaining about!"

At this moment, the final shift occurred. The men no longer needed or depended on the captain's personal leadership. Leadership had progressed from fear to respect and finally to purpose. Now, instead of merely following orders, the men gained something bigger and more important—a true purpose. Instead of blindly following orders, they were united in their aim.

What Leadership Is Responsible For

Direction: How the organization carries out its mission and progressively moves toward a destination.
Purpose: Finding personal fulfillment and meaning in the organization's vision, mission, and goals.
Alignment: The relationship between an individual's attitudes, drives, dreams, goals, and abilities and the needs of the organization.

Good leaders create a clear sense of direction and purpose. They do so by creating an alignment between the individual and the organization. It isn't easy; in fact, it takes plenty of energy and emotion to get people to see how their contributions make a difference to an organization. But clear purpose and direction—clear alignment—is a powerful retention strategy in today's changing workforce.

"What are the reasons you stay at your present job?"

Thirty-nine percent said, "Feel like we have a purpose."

Source: Chart Your Course Workforce Retention Survey.

Figure 3.1   Performance Satisfaction Quotient

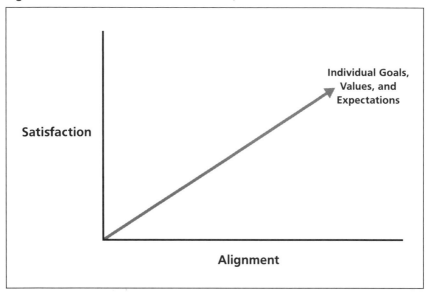

The Performance Satisfaction Quotient

Ask people why they stay with their employer and you may be surprised by their answers. Their response is based on their level of job satisfaction. Every individual has the capacity to perform on a continuum from low to high. I call this the Performance Satisfaction Quotient (PSQ), which is illustrated in Figure 3.1. The greater the alignment between the individual and the organization's needs, the greater the individual's job satisfaction.

In a high-retention organization, the PSQ is fulfilled at work. People enjoy what they are doing and feel their actions are important and appreciated. In a low-retention organization, PSQ is harder to fulfill. In this situation, people seek fulfillment outside work in bowling tournaments, golf, personal relationships, PTA, civic groups, hobbies, family, and artistic endeavors.

In a survey conducted probably 20 years ago, social scientists from Johns Hopkins University asked 7,948 students at 48 colleges to rate what they considered very important to them now. Sixteen percent of the students checked "making a lot of money." Seventy-eight percent said their first goal was "finding a purpose and meaning in life."

It's a manager's job to hire and place people in jobs. However, to place people effectively, managers must attempt to discover workers' motivations and drives, and match their skills to a job that will provide them the greatest satisfaction. The more fulfillment a person finds in life at work, the higher his or her PSQ, and the greater the likelihood that he or she will stay with the organization longer.

What turns someone on varies from person to person and generation to generation. What satisfies a 20-year-old worker may not satisfy a 60-year-old worker. Most adults realize that money is important, but at some point in their life priorities shift. Once financial and physical needs are met, they start looking for a more meaningful life. Managers who are serious about retention and productivity will take the time to discover how their employees define *meaning*.

You're in the Army Now

I joined the U.S. Army's medical department directly out of college. I was on the fast track and my career was moving in a positive direction. But even though I was getting promotions and was financially stable, I didn't feel satisfied with what I was doing.

One day I told my wife I was getting out of the military and going to the seminary. I thought I was called to be a preacher. "Leave a good-paying career for the ministry?" she asked. I wasn't even 30, so I couldn't be having a midlife crisis! For the next several months I did a lot of soul searching and praying. It turned out I wasn't called for the ministry but for something just as important. My calling was to stay in the business world and show business people how to create work environments that provide meaning and purpose to those who work there.

I discovered that I was task oriented, enjoyed a dynamic work environment, and needed to work in a place where I could help others. No wonder I spent so many years in health care, military service, and emergency services. They made me feel good and kept me aligned with my "calling"—the drives in my life that kept me motivated.

In retrospect I can understand why I disliked other jobs I held. The requirements of the job did not match my motivations. In some jobs I was so hamstrung by red tape that it drove me to my limits of frustration—I couldn't make a difference. But other employees were perfectly content in that same work environment. Why?

Everyone is driven differently. We all have a set of drives or attitudes and motivations that are important to us. Unfortunately, most people are not sure what makes them happy, much less which jobs are fulfilling. When they are not happy at home, they will not be happy at work. If they are not happy at work, they will end up with lower productivity and eventually quit or be fired. It isn't because they are fickle—they are in the wrong job.

People who don't understand their own drives or attitudes can become dissatisfied. Because they don't know what they like or what they are good at, they fall into jobs and stay there because of security and a fear of changing. As a result, a business may be filled with unsatisfied, unfulfilled people who are afraid to leave but make everyone else miserable by sticking around. The few people who do understand their strengths and drives rise to the surface and (sometimes) become the top performers.

Three Steps to Creating Meaning and Purpose at Work

People will not give their all until they have alignment with three things:

1. Personal motivations, attitudes, and abilities
2. The requirements and expectations of the job
3. How they see their job making a difference in the world

When these three factors are aligned with the purpose of the business, a psychological connection is created between a worker's soul, mind, and job; and retention and productivity leap.

Creating this kind of purpose takes leadership. I believe it's a manager's job to help people clarify direction and purpose and create meaning at work. In my view, this process involves taking three steps:

1. Discovery
2. Alignment
3. Deployment

Step 1: Discovery

- Why do people see things differently?
- Why are children in the same family so different?
- Why do opposites attract in marriage?
- Why do opposites cause conflict at work?
- Why do some people like challenges whereas others avoid them?
- Why do some people enjoy breaking rules whereas others stick by those same rules?
- Why are some people so easy to make friends with?
- Why are others so difficult to get to know?

I began to find answers to these questions when I started using DISC-based assessments and profiles in my consulting practice.

DISC profiles have their origins in the work of Dr. William Marston, whose book *Emotions of Normal People* (1920) explained how people can be understood and how they fall into four distinct and predictable types or styles of behaviors:

1. D—Dominant
2. I—Interacting

Figure 3.2 Four Quadrants

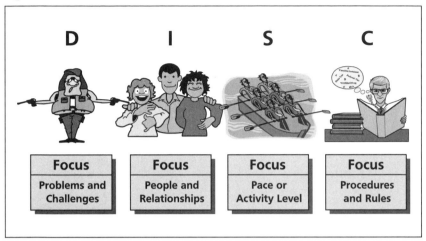

3. S—Steady
4. C—Cautious

Using DISC profiles will help you see people differently. A DISC profile is not a test or an evaluation of goodness and badness. It builds a doorway of communication that allows you to better understand yourself and others. When you understand why people do what they do, you can place them in an environment where they can become a top performer—not to mention a more loyal and productive employee.

These four quadrants shown in Figure 3.2 are further subdivided into eight descriptors as shown in the Success Insights Wheel in Figure 3.3.

In my experience, about 60 percent of turnover results from bad hiring decisions. A DISC profile is the quickest way to understand a person's motivations, abilities, emotional intelligence (EQ), strengths, and limitations. Perhaps you hired someone to fill a customer service job, someone who hated people, or you brought on a manager with no management experience. A DISC profile can't fix a hiring mistake, but it can enable employee and manager to better understand each other in order to create alignment.

Figure 3.3   Success Insights Wheel

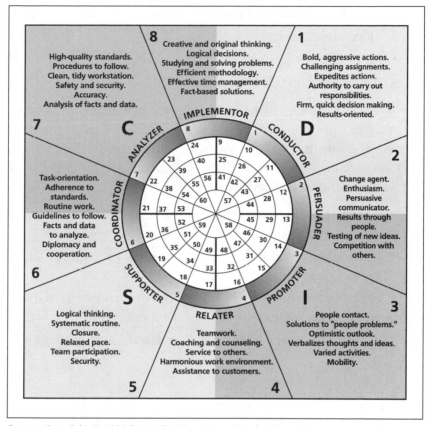

Source: Copyright © 1999 Target Training International, Ltd., and Cassetta Associates.

When I first began using DISC profiles, I was skeptical. But the more I used them, the more confident I became in their validity and the more benefits my clients and I experienced. Helping individuals understand themselves and their behavior patterns and aligning their skills with the right job allow them to become top performers with high job satisfaction. Other benefits of DISC profiles include:

- Better understanding and acceptance of differences
- Higher productivity
- Reduced stress

- Reduced conflict
- Improved communication
- More effective teambuilding
- More effective personal development
- New opportunities for potential

With only 24 short but revealing questions, a DISC assessment takes only ten minutes to administer. The assessment is scored by computer and provides a customized 26-page report that includes a 2-page overview on the individual and his or her value to the organization. The report

- rates the individual on 12 leadership skills/competencies;
- provides a checklist, do's and don'ts, and tips on communicating;
- explains the individual's ideal work environment, natural work styles, and areas of improvement; and
- tells the manager how best to motivate and manage the person.

You can receive a complimentary profile by visiting our Web site: <www.chartcourse.com/ttiassessmts.html>

D-Factor: Dominant, Driver, Director

Business Focus: Problems and Challenges

General Tendencies of the High D
Needs: Control, direct, challenge, win
Looking for: Results
Emotion: Anger/short fuse
Change: Love it!
Conflict: Fight back
Rules: Break them
Read: *Cliff Notes*

Talk on phone: Short
Talk to people: Direct while jumping to next issue
Office: Status symbols

Value to the Team:
- Initiates action
- Innovative
- Goal oriented
- Strategic vision
- Task oriented

I-Factor: Interacting, Inspiring, Sociable

Business Focus: People and Relationships

General Tendencies of the High I
Needs: To talk and be liked
Looking for: People
Emotion: Optimism/trust
Change: Not afraid of change
Conflict: Flight, run
Rules: What rules?
Read: Fiction, self-improvement
Talk on phone: Long conversations
Office: Memorabilia of experiences

Value to the Team:
- Enthusiastic
- Optimistic
- Motivates others toward goals
- Team oriented
- Good at resolving conflicts

S-Factor: Steady, Stable, Service

Business Focus: Pace or Activity Level

General Tendencies of the High S
Needs: To serve
Looking for: Trust
Emotion: Nonemotional (masking)
Change: No change please!
Conflict: Tolerates it
Rules: Follow
Read: Fiction/nonfiction—people stories
Talk on phone: Warm
Office: Family snapshots, "homey"

Value to the Team:
- Dependable
- Empathetic
- Works hard on projects
- Service orientation
- Patient
- Good listener

C-Factor: Cautious, Compliant, Accurate, Analytical

Business Focus: Procedures and Rules

General Tendencies of the High C
Needs: Proof and accuracy
Looking for: Precision
Emotion: Fear
Change: Concerned
Conflict: Avoidance
Rules: "By the book"
Read: Technical journals
Talk on Phone: To the point
Walk: Straight line
Office: Charts, graphs

Value to the Team:
  • High standards
  • Defines, clarifies, and gets information
  • Objective thinker
  • Good problem solver

Steps 2 and 3: Alignment and Deployment

By applying the results of a DISC assessment, you can begin the process of aligning an employee's drives with the company's mission.

This is the very heart of retentionship. Developing people is always cheaper and has more long-term benefits than replacing them. Through a DISC assessment, managers can learn more about their employees and begin training, developing, and helping people maximize their abilities in ways that benefit an organization and make them star performers.

DISC assessments can be very revealing. It told me why one executive-level group was having problems accomplishing its goals: It was because the executive director and two assistant directors were high Is, and their natural inclination was to put more effort into pleasing people and building positive relationships than planning and directing the affairs of the company. To get more direction and make their organization more effective, they needed to rely on outside assistance and place more time and energy in the other three quadrants.

DISC assessments also help coworkers understand how to get along better. I've found that while opposites attract in marriages, on the job people like to work with similar people. DISC assessments help coworkers understand that each person has unique strengths and abilities. People have a tendency to evaluate each other based on their own prejudices and expectations. For example, a person who is slow, methodical, and concerned about quality might look skeptically at another who values speed over quality and works like a bat out of hell. When people can see that a behavior is different but has unique benefits, they can better accept differences.

Without understanding, alignment isn't possible. What happens when goals aren't aligned? I knew a man who always wanted to be in the army but couldn't. Projecting his unrealized dream onto his son, he pushed and pushed his son to go to West Point. After a laborious process, he got his son an appointment to West Point. It was a dream come true for Dad—until his son quit two weeks later. A $50,000 scholarship went down the drain because West Point was in alignment with Dad's drives but not his son's.

Let's look at a couple of companies that have succeeded in creating an alignment between the company's goals and individual goals and deploy their people in ways that use their abilities.

Singapore International Airlines, for one, has improved its retention ratios by placing more time and effort in the selection and training of its employees. Not everyone has the mindset and personality suitable for the service industry. Using behavioral-based interviews and assessments, the company identifies employees with service-oriented personalities and has created a win–win for all concerned. Employees enjoy their jobs more, the company spends less money recruiting, and customers tend to spend more money with companies that offer above-average service.

Flying above Mediocrity: Organizational Alignment at Singapore International Airlines

It was the food cart bashing my knee that woke me from a pleasant dream. As I grabbed my knee, I saw the flight attendant with the "hit-and-run" food cart heading down the aisle.

I was on the final leg of a long trip, flying on a well-known but mediocre domestic airline that was once known for its good service. Only hours before, I had been traveling on Singapore International Airlines (SIA).

SIA is so superior that it leaves other carriers in its vapor trails—even other overseas carriers known for their good service. The positive experience on SIA makes the air passenger's Bill of Rights completely unnecessary.

How does SIA create this experience? It places the needs of passengers first and offers service that is above and beyond the ordinary. Even in economy class, the experience is unforgettable. Pillows and blankets are carefully placed on every seat. Once in the air, smiling attendants offer champagne or orange juice and carefully avoid smashing passengers' body parts with their carts! Passengers are presented with a kit containing a toothbrush, toothpaste, and special socks for the trip. At the beginning and the end of each flight, passengers receive hot towels to freshen up. Particularly pleasing are the individual monitors on the back of each seat where even the most wearied traveler can select from over 15 videos, a telephone, audio programs, Nintendo games, and up-to-the-minute travel information.

All classes enjoy first-class treatment. I don't think I ever saw one peanut on this flight. Passengers are presented with a menu with choices. The food in the back of the plane is better than it is on other carriers' first-class flights. After meals, attendants bring liqueurs, beer, juice, or anything else you want—no charge. I almost wanted to say, "Leave me alone; quit feeding me!"

Singapore Airlines can delight its customers with high-level service because it hires and supports workers who like providing service and feel aligned with the company's overall goals. In a tight labor market, companies are tempted to hire anyone who walks through the door. My experience shows that the more time an organization invests in finding employees who understand and have values, drives, and motivations that match the company's, the more successful the organization becomes. Because SIA has spent extra effort and energy in creating alignment between employees and the company, its top-performing employees have a service orientation and truly find pride in what they do.

How SIA creates alignment is explained in the following paragraphs.

Provides staff training and development. SIA's heavy investment in staff development and training—conducted in good times and bad—enables staff members to stay focused and continuously upgrade their performance. Training and development fights complacency and keeps crew members capable of handling demanding situations. It also gives the airline a distinct advantage. First, it demonstrates that continuous learning and development help people do a better job, which in turn helps individuals improve their potential. Second, it allows SIA to stay ahead of its competition while other carriers may be cutting back.

Embraces change and innovation without fear. SIA is known for innovation. Instead of copying other airlines, it takes the lead. Instead of charging passengers a $5 entertainment fee, it gives away headsets. Instead of charging for drinks, it gives them away along with free postcards and the needed postage. Passengers in the Raffles Class section have seats that recline into beds. SIA benchmarks other service industries, such as hotels and restaurants, to make its service more comfortable, convenient, and creative.

Maintains consistent communication. With over 27,000 staff members representing 25 nationalities, communication is critical. SIA keeps staff informed of important matters through newsletters and publications, regular meetings between management and staff, and a Staff Ideas in Action program that helps new suggestions and ideas move forward for action and improvement. (Communication, an essential element of retention, is covered in Chapter 6.)

Recognizes, reinforces, and rewards the right behavior. Excellent service is a learned behavior that requires constant reinforcement and recognition. Unless an organization develops systems and processes to reward and recognize the behavior it needs for success, it will never get it. (More on this in Chapter 9.) SIA rewards excellent performance with increased pay and promotions but reserves its most prestigious award for superior acts of customer service. The Deputy Chairman's Award, given yearly to people who have managed customer situations with exceptionally selfless acts of service, is a badge of honor coveted by all employees. Winners and their families fly to Singapore for a special dinner; and information about winners and their families is published in the monthly *Outlook* magazine.

Instills that customers always come first.   Customer service directs and guides SIA in all it does. SIA places a priority on quality service. All questions are answered and decisions made based on the needs of the customer. While other airlines cut back on service to make more profits, SIA retains the customers' needs as its first priority. The bottom line for SIA is not the plane, the seat, or the destination. The bottom line is delivering exceptional service and personifying that service.

TRC Staffing: Finding a Challenging Place to Work

Embree Robinson is the founder and president of TRC Staffing, a $200 million temporary help staffing agency with 75 offices in the southeastern United States and on the West Coast. The worker shortage hits this company square in the face, especially when you consider at any time it may have 500 fewer workers than it needs to fill openings for its clients.

Robinson's personal experience shows there is no one way to attract, keep, and motivate his hard-won workforce. According to him, a lot of things have changed in today's workforce, but one thing remains constant: "The company must stand for something and the leadership is what makes it work."

Robinson takes this challenge personally. He stays in touch with his people as much as possible without being a micromanager. He practices a people-centered approach to management and visits about 25 branch offices a quarter. During each visit he sits down with the branch managers and listens while they discuss their goals, reviews their overall performance, and gives everyone information on how the organization is performing as a whole. During the holiday season, Robinson adds levity by giving out turkeys and Christmas presents while dressed as Santa Claus.

Robinson says that people want two things out of their professional relationship: challenge and security. Challenge means the opportunity to grow professionally as well as financially. Branch managers have the option to buy into the company and become shareholders. The corporate office also rewards each branch office with a hefty 20 percent of the profits. Ten percent goes to the office managers and the other 10 percent is split among branch employees.

To feel secure, people need to know company rules and expectations. They also want their boss to keep them informed about where the company is heading. Workers today want to know the strategic direction of the company, Robinson says. They have ideas and expect upper management to listen to them or they will walk to the next employer who *will* listen and provide the information they need and expect.

Generate Purpose and Direction with a Mission Statement

A mission statement that spells out the company's goals, purpose, and beliefs is an excellent tool for increasing alignment for workers. A good example of a clearly articulated set of values and beliefs that helps create a high-retention culture comes from Earthlink (formerly known as Mindspring), the world's second largest Internet provider. Its clear mission, purpose statement, and set of core values and beliefs put Earthlink in a better position to attract the kind of employee who will thrive in its environment. (See Figure 3.4.) Statements such as "Work

Figure 3.4   Earthlink's Mission Statement

EARTHLINK'S MISSION
To become the leading Internet service provider in the world, as measured by number of members, member satisfaction, and profitability.
OUR PURPOSE
To change the way the world does business by demonstrating what a company based on integrity and respect for the individual can accomplish.
To improve people's lives by giving them the ability to communicate better than ever before.
To enable our employees and shareholders to flourish and prosper.
CORE VALUES AND BELIEFS
We respect the individual, and believe that individuals who are treated with respect and given responsibility respond by giving their best.
We require complete honesty and integrity in everything we do.
We make commitments with care, and then live up to them. In all things, we do what we say we are going to do.
Work is an important part of life, and it should be fun. Being a good businessperson does not mean being stuffy and boring.
We love to compete, and we believe that competition brings out the best in us.
We are frugal. We guard and conserve the company's resources with at least the same vigilance that we would use to guard and conserve our own personal resources.
We insist on giving our best effort in everything we undertake. Furthermore, we see a huge difference between "good mistakes" (best effort, bad result) and "bad mistakes" (sloppiness or lack of effort).
Clarity in understanding our mission, our goals, and what we expect from each other is critical to our success.
We are believers in the Golden Rule. In all our dealings, we will strive to be friendly and courteous, as well as fair and compassionate.
We feel a sense of urgency on all matters related to our customers. We own problems and we are always responsive. We are customer-driven.

is an important part of life, and it should be fun" and "Being a good businessperson does not mean being stuffy and boring" clarify expectations and set a standard for how people should act—an easy and effective way to create alignment.

Prescription | for Action

- Ensure that employees understand the mission, values, and purpose of the organization.
- Allow employees the ability to switch jobs within the organization easily.
- Conduct a comprehensive orientation program for all employees.
- Conduct a DISC profile on employees.
- Take the time to understand the needs, expectations, and motivations of your employees.
- Take more time selecting employees. High retention begins with hiring the right people.
- When hiring people, don't misrepresent the job opportunities available at your organization.
- Allow employees opportunities to participate in volunteer activities outside work.
- Involve all departments in strategic planning.
- Ensure that senior leaders verbalize and demonstrate organizational goals and direction.
- Develop goals in alignment with the strategic plan.
- Identify trends and issues that will have an impact on the organization.

Chapter Four

Become a Better Leader by Showing Me You Care

One morning at the airport, I overheard a new employee talking about her new boss. "He's a nice guy," she said. "He makes me feel good about working here."

Like many employees, this young woman is more influenced by her boss's soft skills than his technical skills. His interpersonal skills were what mattered most: his ability to communicate, motivate, and show genuine concern. These soft skills make people want to keep working for you. When a manager lacks these skills or actively cultivates their hard-edged opposite, workers who have choices will jump ship.

I experienced this myself when I went into the service right after college. My boss was a special person—a great boss. An experienced veteran and a former Special Forces medic in Vietnam, he was the type of person who always put the needs of others before his own.

One night I pulled duty that required me to stay up all night on New Year's Eve. The next morning, when I still had several more hours to go, the phone rang. It was Joe, my boss. He and his wife had made something he wanted to bring over to me. I don't remember the menu, but I've never forgotten the meal. That one small act of kindness showed me he cared. It taught me more about leadership than all the degrees and diplomas hanging on my wall. It confirmed the truth of the old military saying, "If you take care of your troops, your troops will take care of you." It's still true today.

The older I get and the more I see reinforce my attitude that leadership styles change with the times, but caring for people holds constant. Caring for people can't be faked. On the other hand, no manager should be a pushover. A caring manager must also be respected. Soon after my boss treated me to a meal, he gave me the worst chewing out I'd ever had. It hurt more—and made a deeper impression on me—because of the respect I had for him. When you respect someone, you always value what he or she has to say.

Businesses that do a good job selecting, training, and developing their managers will enjoy higher productivity and lower turnover. Although it's hard to measure the impact soft skills have on productivity, I strongly believe that an employee who feels good about working for a company or a boss will want to contribute much more than the minimum acceptable level.

In the years I have led people, I've never viewed people as average, but as people who have the potential to become much better. I think it was General Ulysses S. Grant who said, "There are no bad soldiers, only bad leaders." In the workplace, average workers usually have average managers; exceptional workers have exceptional managers. The only difference between the two groups is the quality of the leader.

I imagine that my first boss saw me as an average officer with a short attention span and young, inexperienced, and scattered. Fortunately for me, he took the time to train and develop me, even though it often frustrated him. He was a true leader. He knew that leadership of people is a transformation process, and with the right tools and a willing attitude, he could make the transformation happen.

"To improve your workplace environment, where would you like to see your managers improve?"

Better at communicating	69%
Set the example	46
Be more appreciative of what I do	39
Don't micromanage	37
Show genuine concern	36
Try new things at work	36
Listen to my ideas	30
Be more fun at work	26

Source: Chart Your Course Workforce Retention Survey.

Counterproductive Actions Used as Substitutes for Leadership

- Generate only e-mail messages and memos.
- Hire a consultant to tell people what they already know.
- Jump on the new management fad.
- Let Human Resources fix it.
- Dilute responsibility and create a new department.
- Take a climate survey and then hide the results.
- Form a committee, study the problem, and then take no action.
- Blame other people for your mistakes.

Leadership Myths That Block High Retention

Many managers are limited by their own self-defeating belief system. Such a belief system is built on popular but misguided ideas about leadership that I call leadership myths. Often, these myths prevent the most qualified people from rising to the top. Let's look at some of the leadership myths that need to be dispelled.

Myth: Leadership is a rare ability given only to a few.
The idea that leaders are born, not made—and that there are
only a few of them—couldn't be further from the truth. Most
people have the potential to become good leaders. Leadership
is not like a diet pill. Like most learned skills, it takes time,
training, and lots of trial by error. The best companies strive to
develop and create as many leaders as possible.

Myth: Leaders are charismatic. Many leaders have charismatic personalities, but closer scrutiny shows that most leaders are not charismatic. Some of the world's most famous
leaders had warts—some shortcoming or personality defect.
Although people skills are more important than technical
skills, the best leaders are those who work toward a goal. Your
cause, your purpose, and your mission in life will make you
charismatic, not just your personality.

**Myth: The person with the highest title, rank, or posi-
tion is the leader.** Authentic leadership is based on action,
performance, ability, and results, not position or rank. Unfortunately, too many people use their position to demoralize and
destroy a business rather than nurture it.

W. L. Gore & Associates, maker of Gore-Tex and other products, practices natural leadership—that is, leadership by follow-
ship. Instead of appointing leaders, it lets the true leaders rise
to the surface. People naturally gravitate to those they want to
follow and work with. There are no limiting job descriptions or
job titles and few rules and regulations. If a person comes up
with a new product idea, he or she puts a team together of people who have the desire and knowledge to make it work.

**Myth: Effective leadership is based on control, coercion,
and manipulation.** Real leadership is based on respect, not
coercion. Good leaders gain followers based on their ability to
motivate people to work toward a particular goal or achieve a
destination. As Joel Barker, author of *Paradigm,* says, "A leader
is someone you would follow to a place you would not go to by

yourself." People follow when they can relate to the vision or goal personalized by the leader.

Myth: Good leaders have more education than other people. When it comes to leadership, experience, not education, is the best teacher. The U.S. military has the best leadership development program in the world. In the military, you start out at the bottom. You are placed in leadership positions and closely evaluated by superiors. As your experience broadens, so does your responsibility. This practical experience is reinforced with weeks and months of formal training throughout an individual's career.

Myth: Leaders cannot share power. This myth is particularly harmful. In our downsized, fast-paced working environment, people must share power and authority. Leaders must learn to be comfortable in chaos. Give away as much of your power as possible and you will accomplish more and sleep better at night.

Competencies Managers Need Today

Executive Level	*Midlevel*
Sense of humor	Flexibility
Provide a purpose and values	Team orientation
Lead by example	Intuition
Communication skills	Ability to teach others
Create a charged work environment	Enthusiasm
Ability to remove barriers and obstacles	Problem-solving skills
Strategic vision	Tactical vision
Ability to unlearn	Ability to learn quickly
Create change	Manage change
Innovation	Manage and sell ideas

Survey Comments: What Employees Want from Their Supervisors

"Stop taking away benefits, etc., and train managers better. Managers of the past continue to do the same things, never try anything new or are not willing to do the extra work to improve matters. Often poor performance is addressed, if at all, over and over again without any consequences. Or worse, addressed once and the person is transferred to another position. This sends a very bad message." (Joseph Alliant, computer specialist)

"Better and more frequent feedback sessions with each employee. Our leadership is good and does care, but the pressures of their day make them less effective communicators than would be possible in a "do less" workplace. Everyone here works hard, but the work never stops and so some very good and great young people reach a saturation point and begin to look for a job with less demanding hours and stress." (Samantha Christian, office manager)

"I'm still struggling with the lack of 'alleged' leadership traits in many executives. How do they achieve executive positions? Why don't they seek out training to develop/enhance their leadership skills? Why do they assume that their subordinates need training but they don't? What actually is the essence of leadership? How can we teach executives to think strategically, to plan, to envision and to leave operational decisions to managers?" (Mary Worth, customer service specialist)

Leaders Who Care: Qiagen NV

Metin Colpan, a Ph.D. in organic chemistry and chemical engineering from Darnstadt Institute of Technology and president of the Dutch biotech firm Qiagen NV, is a leader who cares.

He writes thank-you notes by pen—a thoughtful, caring gesture in today's high-tech world.

He shares his dreams in daily talks with people at all levels of the company and in monthly large-group lunches. He shares his plans and vision for the future and lets people know how their efforts help contribute to society.

He offers associates a stock option plan so everyone can share in the success of the company.

He brings people in from the outside to get fresh perspectives and ideas, which coincidentally prevents company executives from thinking they are "extremely smart and know everything."

Instead of micromanaging, he allows workers to make mistakes. He knows that mistakes are a natural part of the learning process. Of course, he doesn't entirely ignore mistakes but meets with erring individuals to review what has been learned so both he and they can move on.

Colpan's personal and caring leadership generates results. Sales in this firm reached $74 million in 1997. Between 1990 and 1997, Qiagen's earnings grew by an average of 74 percent a year.

Building a Structure of Caring: La Rosa's Pizza Company

Low pay, long hours, working weekends, and a workforce perceived to be of low caliber and/or low skill—these factors add up to constant turnover for the service and food industry, as Figure 4.1 indicates. Because it has the lowest retention and highest turnover of all U.S. industries, many food industry managers are frustrated and, in some cases, reluctant to make fundamental changes to the way they manage people.

One company, however, clearly stands out above the rest: La Rosa's Pizza Company, a national chain with 53 outlets, 3,000 employees, and more than $100 million in sales each year. At the helm of this family-owned business, whose corporate offices are in Cincinnati, Ohio, is nonfamily Chief Executive Officer Tillman "TD" Hughes.

When I met TD at the PizzaExpo conference, he handed me a silver dollar–sized coin bearing a La Rosa's logo and these words: "Good, better, best. Never let it rest until your good is better and your better is best."

La Rosa's practices the art of leadership and takes the science of quality management to its highest form. It stands apart from other food businesses because it considers employees its internal customers. La Rosa's spends as much time and energy

Figure 4.1   Quick Facts about the Food Industry

Food Industry

Typical Employee Profile

58% female
59% younger than 30
71% high school graduates
82% live with parents at home
Works an average of 25.5 hour per week

Employee Turnover:
For full-service operations whose typical checks are less than $10

1997: 88%
1998: 85%

For full-service operations whose typical checks are $10 or more
1997: 61%
1998: 83%

Limited-service food operations
1997: 85%
1998: 117%

Source: Restaurants USA <www.Restaurant.org>.

focusing on its internal customers as its external customers. Taking care of employees is like the law of physics—for every action there is an equal and opposite reaction. In this case, the reaction is a higher level of customer service, which in turn generates higher profits.

According to TD, one of his toughest jobs is getting managers to adopt the mindset that people need as much time and attention as the product. Recently, while working with a new distributor, he realized that La Rosa's spends more time talking to its distributors than its employees. "This is wrong," he told me. "We must communicate more with our new people so they feel more part of the organization. People need to feel good about what they do," he added.

In most businesses, the human resources (HR) department is responsible for people issues. Unfortunately, in most American companies, the HR manager is only a staff position and in many cases lacks the power or respect to make changes. But La Rosa's eliminated its HR department and created a chief people officer. This was no mere name change. Now the responsibility, authority, and power for the internal customers rest with the top executives. As TD puts it, "The soft stuff needs to become the 'hard stuff.'"

The CEO and other senior executives have a people-first philosophy. "I have never found anyone who didn't want to do a good job. You hire for attitude and train for skills," says TD. "You must create a goal for them to reach and then show them how to get from A to B."

Measure What Is Important

To make sure it gives more than lip service to taking care of its employees, La Rosa's uses several different methods to measure its efforts. This puts La Rosa's management in a powerful position for making improvements and holding people accountable.

Managers meet weekly with new hires for the first four weeks and then conduct a new-hire survey. Feedback from new employees reveals how they feel about working there and how their training is going.

Once a year, La Rosa's does a cultural audit, similar to an internal climate assessment, which measures feelings about pay and benefits, care and recognition, and the like. The audit gives management a quick pulse on how employees feel about their treatment.

Employees also evaluate their bosses twice a year in a bottom-up internal customer satisfaction index (ICSI), shown in Figure 4.2. The ICSI has only four questions and asks the employees to give their managers a letter grade from A to D in four categories, as shown.

Figure 4.2   La Rosa's Customer Satisfaction Index Survey

LA ROSA'S, INC.	
INTERNAL CUSTOMER SATISFACTION INDEX SURVEY	

Team Member (Supplier): _____

RATING SCALE

A	TOTAL SATISFACTION WITH TEAM MEMBER PERFORMANCE
B	GENERALLY SATISFIED WITH TEAM MEMBER PERFORMANCE
C	GENERALLY DISSATISFIED WITH TEAM MEMBER PERFORMANCE
D	TOTAL DISSATISFACTION WITH TEAM MEMBER PERFORMANCE

**IF SCORING IS RATED "B" OR LESS, PLEASE EXPLAIN YOUR REASON SO THE TEAM MEMBER KNOWS WHAT NEEDS TO BE IMPROVED.

COMMUNICATION:
Use of basic principles, effective method used/established for verbal and written messages or instructions, feedback provided or allowed—Code of Conduct honored

ACCOUNTABILITY:
Timeliness, maintains schedules, facilitates the work flow, responsiveness

QUALITY:
Provides quality work and/or service (i.e.: accurate info, support documentation, quality products, etc.)

PROFESSIONALISM:
Exhibits courtesy and professionalism. Handles situations in a mature manner. Effectively communicates and delivers quality products/service resulting in total Team Member satisfaction.

COMMENTS: (If additional comment space is required, please attach a second sheet.)
_____
_____
_____
_____
_____

Please return in the envelope provided   Due Date:

"La Rosa's Commitment to Good, Better, Best!"

If an employee gives a manager a grade of B or lower, he or she is asked to provide specific comments so the team member knows what needs to be improved. After the ICSI is completed and the comments tabulated, the CEO has the managers come in and talk about the results.

Together they address specific behaviors and devise action plans for improvement that can be tracked daily. The meetings are held in an open and trusting environment so as not to threaten a fear of retaliation. La Rosa's current initiative is to find out what is keeping it from being staffed at 100 percent. The chief people officer (CPO) is responsible for the initiative.

People Development Charts

To stay focused on people, all managers from the senior vice presidents to the store managers at La Rosa's use a tool called a "people development chart." The chart is a visual tool listing the individual goals, targets, and needed training the managers have identified for themselves during the year.

Leadership training is key to La Rosa's success. At one time managers were sent to public, one-day leadership courses downtown. But critical mass was hard to reach because everyone came back with different ideas, a different philosophy, and a different language explaining what leadership meant. La Rosa's now sends all managers to the same six-week training program, which deals with aspects of their personal life and their professional life. This training is much more effective because it is repeatable and universal. Furthermore, graduates can hold each other accountable.

Standardized training gives managers a common language and a common methodology for solving problems and improving processes, which drives everything La Rosa's does. The slogan "Good, better, best. Never let it rest until your good is better and your better is best" underpins this improvement methodology.

"We view ourselves as a manufacturing company," TD says. "Everything about a restaurant is like a manufacturing com-

pany, but most (restaurant) people think they are different."
Instead of production time, La Rosa's measures delivery time.
Instead of manufacturing facilities, it has kitchens. By focusing on this continuous improvement model, significant
improvements and high retention are much easier to attain.

Don't Take a Tumble: Maintain Trust

Humpty Dumpty sat on a wall
Humpty Dumpty had a great fall
All the King's horses and all the King's men
couldn't put Humpty Dumpty back together again.

What does a nursery rhyme have to do with leadership?
Leadership is about trust, and trust is as fragile as an egg. Once
it is broken or lost, it is almost impossible to get back.

Once upon a time, people trusted their leaders. Trust came
with the job. Today it is different. We are a doubting and mis-
trustful society. Reason: people in positions of authority vio-
lated their pact with those they were supposed to lead. Their
personal lives stained their public lives. I was always taught to
avoid all appearance of evil. Obviously, not everyone takes
that advice and we suffer the consequences.

The bottom line is that it doesn't matter if you are the president of the United States or the store manager of the local
pharmacy—you must build trust to be an effective leader.

Here are some ways to keep and build trust:

- *Don't forget that your personal life is your public life.*
  Your personal life is a reflection of who you really are. If
  you are in a leadership position, your personal life is
  open to public scrutiny. People will not follow you if
  they do not respect you. You may not like it, but that is
  the way it is.

- *Tell the whole story.* The worst thing you can do is not
  be open and honest with people. Trying to hide information will always bite you in the posterior. Tell people

everything they need to know, even if it's bad news. It's better to say too much rather than too little.

- *Do what you say you will do.* How many times has someone told you, "I'll get back to you on that," but never followed up? Don't make promises you can't or won't keep. Trust breaks down when promises are broken.

- *Listen to others.* Give people 100 percent of your attention. Seek first to understand. Repeat back what you think they are telling you. Don't be one of those people who seem more interested in something else or someone else during the conversation.

- *Treat others with respect and dignity.* Whose interests do you support first—yours or theirs? People will trust you if you put their interests first. Surprise people by doing something unexpected for them. I used to send hand-written notes to my employees when I saw them doing something good.

- *Avoid favoritism.* Don't turn to the same person for help again and again, or send all the perks and challenges in the same direction. Good leaders give everyone an opportunity to shine by training and developing all their employees. If employees refuse to shine or take the responsibility, find them a job somewhere else.

- *Don't make jokes at others' expense.* Telling jokes is a good way to lower your trust quotient. No matter how simple or funny they are, someone may be offended. Even *Dilbert* cartoons hurt credible management. They create a perception that all managers are stupid.

- *Consistently enforce the rules.* Eliminate unnecessary rules, regulations, and policies, and enforce all the rest. When you don't consistently enforce policies, you will gradually lose trust. Everyone in the business has a different perception of the rules. What appears an unnecessary rule to you is important to someone else. Either enforce it or eliminate it.

- *Seek others' ideas and opinions.* The biggest complaint I hear from employees: "My supervisor won't listen to my ideas." Improve your standing by asking their opinions. Even if those opinions run counter to yours, they will respect you more for listening. You never know when someone else's idea may save your job or improve the bottom line.

I have noticed from working overseas that a building of trust and respect carries more weight than benefits and pay packages. My experience in Russia showed that the workforce would stay no matter how bad things were simply because there was nothing else to go to.

Many companies would neglect to pay their employees for months on end, knowing that they would still turn up for work so that their "work" record would not have an interruption. Of course, the quality of work and output were so below the norm that these companies had to hire more personnel than required as well as place management at every corner to ensure things were accomplished and to prevent sabotage of the companies' assets.

The difference one could make by not only paying people for the work they performed but also showing there was trust between management and the employees was so enormous it cannot be put in words.

To retain a productive workforce, you have to lead by example, trust in others, and gain the trust and respect of the majority (if not all), or you will be in a continuous state of training replacements.

(48-year-old survey respondent, director, facilities management)

God, Car Batteries, and Concern for the Family: Interstate Battery

In my mind, a good boss is someone who acknowledges important life-changing events such as a death in the family, the birth of a child, or an illness. In one of my scrapbooks is a note from my father's boss congratulating him on my birth. Today, some might call this intrusive or outside the bounds of normal business, but it meant a lot to my family. And I know that similar gestures I've made to people who worked for me made a lasting impression that no bonus check could ever buy.

The modern workforce is in a stressful place. What has traditionally been considered work and what is considered living are becoming difficult to distinguish. Lack of job security, fractured marriages, fear, anxiety, office violence, nonstop change—all these issues are making people realize that life is more than just making money. People need an anchor in their life they may have never needed before. A good boss alone may not be enough.

At the Interstate Battery System of America, Inc. (IBSA), employees can turn to their employer for help in the quest for meaning. Founded in 1952 on three traditional values—offer the best-quality product, provide impeccable service, and treat the customer with respect—Interstate Battery is a $500 million, privately held corporation with more than 5,000 products. Its home office in Dallas works with more than 300 wholesale distribution centers that service 200,000 dealers in the United States, Canada, and around the rest of the world.

Interstate undertakes a unique role and responsibility for its employees and family members. Management tries to make a substantial difference in people's lives beyond merely providing a place to work and a paycheck at the end of the month. Many organizations talk about caring for their employees, but Interstate demonstrates it in a number of ways.

The most notable example is its chaplain's department. Its staff of five provides and coordinates opportunities for employees to participate in pizza luncheons, men's and women's luncheons, banquets, golf tournaments, family life conferences, and summer camps. Employees can borrow books and videos from its library, attend Bible studies, listen to guest speakers, and turn to the department for personal help.

A full-time chaplain has been on Interstate's staff for the past nine years. A former army chaplain who left the service to work at Interstate, he has helped establish many of Interstate's employee programs. The chaplain will visit family members in the hospital, attend weddings, and respond to births and deaths. His office will send newly married employees to family life conferences and pick up half the tab. Employees who participate in these programs view them as a valuable aspect of working at Interstate.

Faith plays a key role at Interstate, whose mission statement calls on the company to "glorify God as we supply our customers worldwide with top quality, value-priced batteries, related electrical power-source products, and distribution services." Norm Miller and other top executives hold regular prayer meetings as part of their management responsibilities and look to God for guidance in day-to-day business decisions.

Employees participate in a variety of volunteer ministries. Every quarter, about 10 spend a weekend in Bill Glass Prison Ministries' "Weekend of Champions." Interstate pays for participants' transportation, food, and lodging. Twice a year, employees donate boxes of food and bags of clothing to the needy at the Union Gospel Mission. At Christmas and Easter, about 17 people participate in a prison fellowship and spend time visiting with inmates in a nearby jail.

Once a year, 100 employees participate in the Angel Tree project, which provides clothing and Christmas presents to children of prisoners. An annual mission trip to Mexico draws about 20 employees; Chairman Miller pays for the trip out of his own pocket.

Interstate recognizes employees who participate in ministry events with a Matthew 25 certificate based on the Bible verse that says, "For I was hungry and you gave Me something to eat; I was thirsty and you gave Me drink; I was a stranger and you invited Me in; I was naked and you clothed Me; I was sick and you visited Me; I was in prison and you came to Me."

It's hard to objectively measure how these programs and services impact on retention and productivity. But evidence indicates that employees feel that Interstate truly stands for something and cares for them. This environment is not for everyone, but for the 350 home office employees, it's ideal. As one new employee said, "I can't get over it, I feel I am a part of a family."

Best Practices | for Caring Management

Recognize and reward workers for their accomplishments. Take time to acknowledge the worth of entry-level employees. However, avoid shallow or routine praise given simply because "that's what the book says to do." Employees, especially older ones, quickly recognize routine praise, which can do more harm than good.

Compliment employees according to the level of their skills. An inexperienced employee may deserve and appreciate a compliment in a situation where an experienced employee would actually scoff at a compliment for something so routine. Tailor your praise (and criticism) to the person and his or her level of expertise.

Consider chaplaincy services. The 500 chaplains of Marketplace Ministries, representing 23 different denominations and faiths, including Judaism and Buddhism, are available 24 hours a day to client companies who want to provide spiritual assistance to employees as well as employee assistance programs to the company. They even go to the hospital to visit family members in need. In 1997, Marketplace Ministries chaplains performed more than 300 weddings and 50 funerals in 1997.

Take time to know your employees as individuals. Get to know your employees on a more personal level so you will better understand what motivates them. Use that knowledge so everyone benefits.

Show what you mean. Adrall E. Pearson, chairman and CEO of Tricon Global Restaurants Inc., owners of Kentucky Fried Chicken, has changed his leadership style from "exhortation to execution." He says, "It's no longer enough to be an idea-driven leader—you need to be a hands-on leader. These days, I spend a lot less time exhorting people to behave differently and a lot more time showing them how."

Prescription | for Action

- Hold individual managers accountable for retention in their departments.
- Be able to tell people how their job individually impacts on the overall company mission.
- Make it part of the company culture to put managers and staff in the field to work with front-line workers at least one day a month.
- Promote managers whose behavior is consistent with the organization's values and philosophies.
- Communicate plans to all employees.
- Terminate or reassign managers/supervisors whose behavior is inconsistent with the organization's vision and values.

Chapter Five

Flexible Benefits Build a More Loyal and Productive Workforce

Benefits used to mean health insurance, vacation time, and a pension plan. Today they can signify everything from flextime to concierge services . . . from day care to dry cleaning . . . from tuition reimbursement to sabbaticals.

As Chapter 1 stressed, today's workers prize flexibility above all else. According to the *Randstad North American Employee Review,* only 34 percent of American employees now prefer a traditional full-time job. As lives grow more complex, people want greater flexibility. That's why the majority of American workers prefer nontraditional jobs where they can work at home, work part-time, or drop in and out of the workforce. Especially for employees juggling the demands of work and family—be those young children or aging parents—employers that offer jobs with flexibility and control are highly desirable.

Even workers with fewer responsibilities want flexibility. Young workers value time for education and development. Besides health insurance and adequate pay levels, older workers want time for friends, family, and travel. It follows, then, that to attract and keep a good workforce, a company must offer benefits that are competitive, flexible, and customized to the individual needs of the employee.

Proof of the importance of flexibility can be seen in a story from consulting firm Ernst & Young, which not long ago was battling high turnover. Of its 34,000 professionals, 23 percent of its women and 18 percent of its men left each year. Many of these departures, which cost thousands of dollars to fill, were blamed on the struggle to balance work and home life. Because more women than men quit every year, the struggle was assumed to be a women's issue.

To combat the problem, the company formed solution teams to evaluate and question Ernst & Young's work culture. Teams quickly discovered that unwritten rules demanded that employees work weekends, stay late, and check e-mail on vacations—all demands that had an impact on the life-balance equation for all employees, not just women. Especially when professionals were married to professionals, demanding work schedules caused frustration and marital difficulties.

To get a handle on the situation, Ernst & Young created and staffed an Office of Retention to improve the work life of all employees. Next, it put together a steering team to tackle the problem. During initial brainstorming, the team debated opening a day care center. Some considered this only a "Band-Aid" approach. Further discussion resulted in three key changes:

1. People were allowed to telecommute.
2. Leaders were asked to set the example by working the same reasonable schedules and not working weekends, staying late, and the like.
3. An evaluation and feedback process was launched.

In addition, every day was declared a casual day, and employees were told not to check voice mail and e-mail while on vacation. Although these changes sound minor, they had a major impact on the demanding work culture at Ernst & Young. Estimates show that retention improved by 15 percentage points in offices located at Palo Alto and San Jose.

Ernst & Young's experience proved a point I've seen again and again in my many years as a management consultant: for some workers, flexibility is as important as, or sometimes more important than, money. Money is great for young people just starting out and for older people salting away retirement funds. But for everyone in between saddled with multiple responsibilities, flexibility is the premium benefit.

Good Benefits Equal High Retention

The high-retention workplace provides a combination of both hard and soft benefits that allows increased flexibility and productivity. Productivity and retention go hand in hand. Allowing employees to become more productive will ensure they stay with you longer. Together, these benefits promote a work environment that builds greater loyalty. For high-retention workplaces, the sky's the limit when it comes to inventing creative new benefits. Consider these:

- IBM employees in Atlanta can wear cutoffs and sandals to work.
- Employees at SAS in North Carolina's Research Triangle have unlimited sick leave and on-site health care for their entire family.
- Employees at Tech Data Corporation in Tampa, Florida, enjoy meals prepared by an executive chef.
- A pizza company takes its management team on an annual hunting trip.
- Blueprints for Electronic Arts (Canada) Inc.'s new facility include a 70-seat movie theater.
- A construction equipment dealership in Louisville, Kentucky, gives employees' children a $50 savings bond for an all-As report card.
- John Nuveen & Company pays for most of its employees' children's college tuition.
- Workers at Netscape in Mountain View, California, can bring their dogs to work!

Benefits have increased in importance to help counterbalance the complex needs and wants of the workforce. In 1960, businesses spent $23.7 billion on benefits. In 1980, they spent $266 billion, and in 1994 businesses increased their spending on benefits to $747 billion. With unemployment recently at an all-time low, workers have much greater latitude in choosing who to work for. Smart employers are realizing that the plain vanilla, take-it-or-leave-it approach may diminish their ability to attract good workers as well as lead current employees to question their own loyalty and dedication to stay.

Benefits have a lot to do with loyalty, even though the concept has changed. Once, loyalty meant lifelong commitment to the organization, no matter what. Today, people view their loyalty as transferable—portable. Loyalty lasts as long as an employee feels the organization is providing for his or her needs.

Although loyalty continues to be important—95 percent of the respondents in my survey rated loyalty important, very important, or highly important—it's time to replace the word *loyalty* with *dedication*. Even though no longer blindly loyal to their organization, people are equally dedicated to their task, their mission, and their team. Customized and competitive benefits can only strengthen their sentiments, whereas indifferent benefits can weaken them. Respondents in my survey rated benefits (48 percent) and flexibility in work hours (45 percent) among the top five reasons for staying at their present job.

Good Benefits Equal High Productivity

A good benefits program not only increases retention and creates more dedicated workers; it generates higher productivity that should positively influence the bottom line. Consider the following:

- Employees who like where they work will help the company make more money. An 800-store survey conducted by Sears showed that when employee attitudes improved by 5 percent, customer satisfaction jumped 1.3 percent, consequently increasing revenue by one-half a percentage point. Employee attitudes do have an impact on the bottom line!

- First Tennessee National Corporation started taking family issues seriously and made them top priority. It reshaped the rules it had forced employees to live under, added many family-friendly new benefits, and sent managers through three and a half days of training. Employees stayed twice as long—and the bank kept 7 percent more of its customers. Furthermore, changes in employee benefits helped contribute to a 55 percent profit gain over two years.

- Aetna Life & Casualty Company reduced resignations of new mothers by 50 percent when it extended its unpaid parental leave policy to six months, saving the company $1 million a year in training, recruiting, and hiring expenses.

Soft Benefits versus Hard Benefits

The type of individual you want to attract and keep drives the quality and quantity of the benefits you should provide.

Although benefits are important, challenging job assignments, salary, and interesting work matter more to employees. Even the finest benefits will leave employees dissatisfied if pay is not competitive. First, focus on paying your employees well and creating a stimulating, rewarding environment. Next, improve the quality of the relationship between employees and their supervisor. A poor relationship creates conflict, and resulting low productivity eventually persuades a good employee to leave. When pay and good relationships are in place, turn your attention to benefits.

A survey from Randstad North America and Roper Research demonstrates the impact that hard and soft benefits have on people staying with their current job. When asked,

"Would you consider staying in current job rather than switch, if . . ."

Hard Benefits

You have health insurance/benefits	70%
You receive competitive industry wages	59
Your workplace provides on-site/internal training	50
Your workplace provides opportunity for outside training opportunities	45
Your workplace provides a stock/profit-sharing program	38
Your workplace gives bonuses based on company profits	37
Your workplace provides college tuition reimbursement	37
Your workplace has an employee award/ recognition program	30
Your workplace provides creative incentives, such as trips or gift certificates	24

Soft Benefits

You like the team of people you work with	71%
There is a pleasant work environment	68
Your workplace is close to home or you have an easy commute	68
The work you do is challenging	65
You have job security where you work	65
Your workplace gives you the opportunity to work independently	59
Your workplace provides opportunity for advancement	55
Your workplace offers flexible work hours	54

Unfortunately, even though most employers acknowledge that benefits and workplace flexibility are important issues, that acknowledgment goes only so far. The *Heldrich Work Trends Survey on Americans' Attitudes about Work, Employers and the Government* pinpointed eight areas employees say are important and measured the percentage of employers who actually provide those benefits and services. Figure 5.1 shows the gap between what employees want and employers provide.

Figure 5.1   Provision of Employee Benefits according to Their
Importance to Employees

Benefit Option	Rated Important by Employee*	Provided by Employer
Opportunity to telecommute	46%	17%
Flexible work hours	87	61
Flexible work days	87	48
Tuition reimbursement	69	33
Unpaid leave	90	74
On-site child care	49	12
Athletic facilities at work	42	21
Emergency time off	91	83

Source: Heldrich Work Trends Survey (Winter 1999) showing the difference between what employers provide and what employees expect.
*Note: Scores were consolidated by combining responses of "extremely important, very important, and somewhat important."

I stay at my company because I have stock options that I am waiting to vest. My company is very strict—8 to 5 hours, no flextime, no working from home, no spending on anything frivolous. It is difficult to motivate the people who work for me when my hands are tied by what I can do. I can't even order lunch for them during a meeting. The company is large with good revenues ($140 billion); they could afford to do some little things to help. They are building a new corporate campus and are going to charge for covered parking. Where we are located now, covered parking is free. (Jamie Johnson, program manager)

Figure 5.2 IT Benefits

Company	Job Benefits	Best Perks
Aspen Consulting <www.asp.com> 847-357-1290	• Unlimited training opportunities • Travel opportunities • Family and team-oriented environment • Aspen incentive program	• Monthly, quarterly, and yearly awards incentive program • End-of-the-year profit-sharing program
Windriver Systems <www.windriver.com> 800-545-9463	• Five weeks' sabbatical after five years of employment • Fifteen paid holidays • Flexible spending account for medical and dependent care expenses • Adoption assistance • Commuter checks to reimburse travel expenses • Short-term and long-term disability	• Stock purchase plan • Three weeks of paid vacation during first year • Tuition reimbursement
InterAccess Co. <www.interaccess.com> 312-496-4200	• Challenging work • Solid working relationships	• Stock options • Transit checks • Company parties • Beer-and-pizza Fridays

Benefits That Attract and Keep IT Workers

IT workers want to be on the leading edge, not the bleeding edge. They want to work with companies that invest in the latest technology, because technology changes so rapidly that they must continually update their skills to avoid becoming obsolete. For this group, cutting-edge technology and generous training and tuition reimbursement are highly appreciated benefits.

IT professionals also appreciate workplaces that accommodate their working styles. They don't like bureaucracy and are not fond of the status quo. They cringe at multiple layers of approval and prefer to get things done quickly. Traditional hierarchies turn them off; flat, nonhierarchical organizations are more appealing. A work environment that keeps them informed and grants considerable autonomy will help motivate and retain IT professionals.

Any company interested in attracting and retaining IT workers should investigate offering benefits and perks like the ones shown in Figure 5.2. Other strategies that help retain IT staff:

- Explain the big picture and how it influences their work and growth.
- Provide specific feedback on IT employees' performance; mention a particular situation or activity.
- Make sure they understand the company's expectations.
- Involve IT employees in the decision-making process whenever possible.
- Listen to their ideas and suggestions.
- Give them room to do the job without unnecessary restrictions.
- Pay for IT employees to attend workshops and seminars.
- Offer on-site classes where IT employees can learn new skills or improve old ones.
- Challenge them with lots of responsibility.
- Assign them a coach or mentor to help their development.

Family-Friendly Benefits That Attract and Keep Working Women

In 1997 the AFL-CIO, whose membership includes 5.5 million women, completed a landmark study on issues affecting working women. The survey included over 50,000 union and non-union women in every occupation and included special samplings of African American, Hispanic, and Asian American women. The following eight conclusions stand out from the survey:

1. Despite the media attention on America's recently booming economy, working women feel job security has deteriorated. Forty-one percent think job security has worsened for women in the past five years compared with 26 percent who think it has improved.

2. Families depend on working women. Sixty-four percent report that they provide about one-half or more of their household income. Of married women, 52 percent contribute about one-half or more of their household income.

3. Good benefits are as critical as good wages in providing economic security. Eighty-seven percent ranked affordable health insurance important; and 79 percent say pension and retirement benefits are very important.

4. Equal pay remains an urgent concern. Almost one-third say their present job does not provide equal pay for equal work—a major issue involving retention and the overall attitude women have toward their jobs.

5. Working women who work part-time are especially concerned about their pay and benefits. Forty percent of the part-timers bring home one-half or more of their family's income. Over half of these women do not have paid vacations, while 83 percent of full-time women do. Only 45 percent have health insurance and 48 percent have paid sick leave. Finally, only 49 percent have pensions of any kind in their current job.

6. Working women who have family responsibilities want greater control over their time so they can better balance their responsibilities. Most believe it is very important to have paid sick leave (82 percent), paid vacation time (76 percent), paid family leave (70 percent), and flexible hours (61 percent). African American women (47 percent) and Hispanic women (50 percent) are the most likely to want child care.

7. In spite of what they want, 42 percent say they do not have paid family leave, 39 percent lack flexible hours, 29 percent do not have sick leave, and 21 percent do not have paid vacation time.

8. Lack of respect stands out as a key issue. Women who are dissatisfied with their jobs are three times as likely as other working women to mention lack of respect as the biggest problem facing women at work. The fear of sexual harassment is included in this category. Over one-third of the women surveyed feel their current employers do not provide adequate protection and punishment of offenders.

Women in the Workplace

- Women consider making time for their family a priority.
- Women are more comfortable sharing information than are men.
- Women are better at building relationships and maintaining harmony in the workplace.
- Women are more in tune with the work environment.
- Women are good team builders.

Flexible Work Arrangements Promote Productivity

Balancing work and family has received a lot of attention over the years, but the truth is that this is more smoke than fire. People work longer hours in downsized and supercompetitive work environments that pressure people to place family in a secondary position. Many workers feel they must choose between work and family. Either they must conform to get promotions or sidestep their career for the family—a tough and bitter pill to swallow. It's no wonder thousands of good people leave good jobs to take lower-level, lower-paying, more accommodating jobs elsewhere. This dilemma has fueled the dramatic rise of home-based and female-owned businesses in the United States.

By creating what I call a flexible work arrangement (FWA), companies can keep good employees without forcing them to sacrifice family life. An FWA will help workers benefit personally and professionally and result in a workforce that is more loyal, committed, and productive.

FWAs provide more options to employees who don't want or need a standard work schedule. A properly prepared FWA allows greater flexibility in balancing roles at work and home. It can also help prevent valuable employees from quitting and taking a less suitable position elsewhere. Most of the time an FWA involves fewer work hours and possibly a proportional reduction of pay and benefits.

A survey by a consulting company, Flexible Resources, of more than 500 women seeking flexible work arrangements found that 64 percent of them either quit or were planning to quit because of the lack of flexible hours. More alarming was that 59 percent of these women never asked their employers to modify their work schedules because they assumed they would be denied or would lose stature. (Younger women are more assertive in seeking flexible work arrangements than are older women; 72 percent of women between 25 and 35 were willing to request an FWA compared with only 30 percent of the respondent women aged 36 to 45.)

Among those who requested, but were denied, a flexible work arrangement, stated reasons for the refusal ran the gamut as follows:

- We can't give it to you and not the others (52%).
- You will not be available to others (48%).
- We have never done it before (24%).
- You won't be as productive as you were when you worked full-time (8%).
- Your job is not conducive to flexible hours (5%).
- There is too much work to do (5%).
- It wouldn't fit into a team atmosphere (5%).

But FWAs have drawbacks. People feel that physical presence equals more opportunity for promotions and advancement. Men are particularly vulnerable to the stigma that you are not competitive if you are not at work full-time.

Working Mother magazine has recognized the innovative work/life programs provided by the Bank of America. Its Child Care Plus program pays eligible workers $35 a week per child for employees earning less than $30,000 a year. After learning that turnover for participants was about half of the peer group not participating, the company expanded the program to include workers with family incomes up to $60,000 and began to allow workers two paid hours a week to participate in their children's school activities. Finally, Bank of America gives $2,000 a year to each employee enrolled in undergraduate college classes and $4,000 for graduate study. As a result, it was able to reduce turnover by 50 percent.

Better Parenting Skills Create a Better Workplace

Most work/life benefit programs address only issues at work. In creating a high-retention workplace, businesses must consider initiating a new paradigm that goes beyond old boundaries clarifying where responsibility begins and ends in the employer-employee relationship. In Conyers, Georgia, several businesses have put to good use the Parent Project, an innovative, little-known program sponsored by the Rockdale Council for the Prevention of Child Abuse (CPCA). The Parent Project addresses the heart of the work/life balance—how to be an effective parent.

The Parent Project is an hour-long, lunchtime program designed for the workplace. It is a nationally recognized parent support and education program, customized to meet the needs of each hosting workplace and its employees. Designed to be easily accessible, convenient, and rewarding to participants, the Parent Project helps employees cope with the heavy demands of balancing work and family life. The council offers a basic eight-week (one hour per week) program with the availability of an advanced four-week follow-up course. The course seeks to help parents

- build close, loving family relationships;
- communicate effectively;
- use positive discipline methods;
- nurture self-esteem;
- understand family roles and responsibilities;
- manage stress;
- exchange information about child care resources; and
- manage time.

Parents who complete the program report better relationships with their children. They also show lower levels of stress, gain greater knowledge and skills in parenting, and have a more positive attitude about their employer. Social support networks formed in parenting classes lessen the effects of work and family stress and contribute to well-being. And businesses see lowered absenteeism and fewer medical insurance claims.

Launched in 1997, the Rockdale CPCA has presented the Parent Project to employees at AT&T, Lithonia Lighting, QSP Distribution Center, Inc. (subsidiary of Reader's Digest), BioLab, and Kysor/Warren. Evaluations have been outstanding. Two of the companies have formed a parent support network with ongoing meetings, which is one of the Parent Project's goals.

Teleasa Foster, former human resources manager at QSP, had an "overwhelming positive response" from the 30 employees who went through the Parent Project program. It has helped her employees establish their priorities more productively, make better choices, and balance work and family life. According to Teleasa, the program has boosted morale overall and created goodwill "beyond measure" between employees and management.

Breast Pumps and Lactating Rooms for Working Mothers

A new trend for many larger organizations is providing the facilities for mothers to use breast pumps and the time to nurse their babies during work. For the past decade organizations have been doing more to bring mothers back to work. With the increasing worker shortage, more organizations are bending over backwards to make the work environment more supportive to mothers and their children.

Statistics from the Department of Labor show that more than half of working mothers with children under the age of one have returned to work. In contrast, only 35 percent returned to work in 1980. At present, only 7 percent of the biggest organizations offer lactation programs, according to a study by Hewitt Associates.

When CIGNA started a breast-feeding pilot program, more than 1,600 working mothers returned from maternity leave to use the program. Studies show that children who breast-feed are healthier and have a lower number of respiratory problems, infections, bacterial meningitis, diarrhea, and pneumonia. Health care officials recommend that babies be breast-fed for their first six months.

CIGNA has offered many work/life programs to its employees. As a result of its lactating-rooms, the company estimates it has saved $240,000 a year in health care–related costs and is said to have saved $60,000 a year by reducing absenteeism among its working mothers.

USAA and the Los Angeles Department of Water and Power

Alongside a serene 20-acre lake in Tampa, Florida, stands the regional office of the United States Automobile Association (USAA), a private insurance company catering to people affiliated with the military services. With 24,000 employees worldwide, USAA has been singled out for providing one of the best

work environments in the Tampa area. In fact, *Fortune* magazine has selected USAA as one of the "Top 100 Best Companies
to Work for in America."

Tom Draude is the regional senior vice president responsible for the 1,700 employees who work in Tampa. He has a re-
freshing management philosophy: "The employees' problems
are our problems," he says. What strikes you about Draude is
that you can feel he cares about the people there. Everyone is
on a first-name basis. After long weekends or times when the
workforce has to respond to a crisis situation, something happens that you don't often see in corporate America. During
"Drinks with Draude," Tom pushes a cart around the building
passing out Danish pastry and sodas, soft drinks, or coffee to
the workers as they handle claims and other matters on their
phones.

This former Marine Corps general also "walks his talk" and
helps to provide state-of-the-art benefits. The 38-hour flextime
program fits all lifestyles. A medical facility provides employees with allergy injections and medications; quiet rooms
accommodate nursing mothers; and an on-site fitness center
lets employees de-stress with weight lifting, aerobics classes,
or appointments with a massage therapist who comes twice a
week for a small fee. Families take advantage of the day care
facility just across the street.

Education and learning are valuable parts of the USAA culture. After one year of employment, all full-time employees are
eligible for tuition assistance. At the corporate campus in San
Antonio, nearly 300 instructors teach many different courses.
In addition, approximately 60 classes are taught by six different colleges in USAA classrooms.

Tom Draude's caring approach to leadership even extends
to resignations. He conducts a personal exit interview with
everyone who leaves his company. During the interview he
makes three points: (1) he sincerely thanks the person for
working at USAA; (2) he says he or she is always welcome to
come back, no questions asked; (3) he asks if there is anything
else they wish to share.

Draude says his second statement occasionally brings tears of thankfulness and relief to employees' eyes, and many employees do return when they realize that the grass is not greener on the other side. At USAA, as at other organizations, many employees do not realize how good they have it until they leave. It is important for employers to constantly make their people aware of their own benefits.

Good workplaces are not limited only to the private sector. The Los Angeles Department of Power and Water (LADPW) offers its 11,000 employees the following:

- A free seven-week lunchtime series on nutrition and pre-natal care
- An ob-gyn/pediatric nurse who comes two days a week to answer medical questions
- Electric nursing pumps for mothers to provide milk to babies at the child care facility (and dads can take the devices home to their partners)
- Certified social workers to help employees use programs and resources
- Parenting classes at lunchtime
- Support groups for parents
- Four-month maternity and paternity leaves
- A resource center for parents and a beeper that lets an expectant father know when his wife goes into labor

---

"Flex schedules for working moms? We have bosses who can come and go as they please, but working moms basically get put in a position where they have no choice but to quit; i.e., pay cut, forced part time, and no option for working at home. These women happen to be some of our best staff, yet our receptionist, who runs a second business from the office and works as she pleases, has complete job security!? (Three of the last four people who left the company were working moms.)"
(32-year-old survey respondent, administrative assistant)

Office Design and Employee Retention

Think office space design has nothing to do with employee retention? Think again. Research by the American Society of American Designers (ASAD) confirms that office space design has an impact on job satisfaction and employee retention. In a survey by the ASAD, 51 percent surveyed said the physical workplace influences them to stay in a job; 41 percent said the physical workplace influences them to take a new job; 22 percent said the physical workplace affects their ability to be happy and comfortable at work; and 21 percent said the physical workplace influences their decision to accept or to leave a job.

Too often, office space design hinders communication and collaboration. Many businesses departmentalize and compartmentalize themselves to the point where the walls and barriers do more than just divide space—they divide people. Dilbert cartoons and terms like *cubefarm* and *hoteling* reveal how workers feel about a depersonalized environment that attempts to organize them and their work life.

As management begins to recognize that office design plays a big role in attracting and keeping a good workforce—not to mention keeping it productive—office design is moving away from mere functionality or "housing" employees. The new holistic approach considers all aspects of design and seeks to create an open work environment where people feel unrestricted and can easily contact those who work around them while still maintaining privacy. In some organizations it's becoming a key factor in determining whether a person joins or leaves the workforce.

Monster.com is a good example of today's trend. There is nothing ordinary about its corporate offices. The ten-foot-tall, green fictional mascot "Trumpasaurus," the wild colors, and the recreation areas where people can play Ping-Pong and video games and use exercise equipment tell everyone that this 75,000-square-foot corporate office is a different place to work.

Lighting distinguishes private spaces from common work areas. Workstations are joined in a zigzag pattern to facilitate easy communication among team members. Everyone has a fully adjustable chair, desk, and keyboard, and all workstations and chairs have wheels so that team members can be grouped quickly for various meetings and gatherings. And the Monster Den, the main common area, includes meeting space for the entire company and a café; other meeting areas are scattered throughout the company's single-floor space.

Monster.com's office was designed outrageously for a specific purpose: attracting the best and brightest IT talent available. "We created an imaginative and interactive environment that helps us achieve our business objectives," says Jeffrey Taylor, Monster.com's founder and CEO. It's working: employees see their environment as a perk that separates their company from the rest and acknowledge that it plays a major part in their decision to work there.

As a manufacturing plant, Wainwright Manufacturing found office design a little more challenging. Don Wainwright felt that if he could walk down to the shop floor and see anyone he wanted, then the employees should have the same right. So Wainwright took down all office walls and replaced them with glass walls, creating a work environment that promotes trust and openness.

At Weather Channel's corporate offices in Atlanta, a team of industrious employees rearranged their cubicles by turning them inward so they could see each other. The new configuration improved productivity and communication as well as employees' ability to respond to what was going on about them.

Successful office design is aligned with four key words: collaboration, connection, comfort, and communication. Herman-Miller, the "parent" of the cubicle, has designed furniture that incorporates these four Cs. Called Resolve, it allows people to maintain their personal identity and privacy while improving productivity. It replaces squares and sharp 90-degree angles with 120-degree turns that eliminate the boxed-in feeling of cubicles. Instead of walls, it features panels that roll on wheels—sort of like flower petals that open for community use and close for privacy. Everything is adjustable to the size, shape, and fit of the worker, who gets more control and freedom over his or her workspace.

Steelcase, Inc., the world's largest office furniture manufacturer, has taken this approach (the four Cs) even further with their Pathways portfolio of interior products. Pathways is an evolving product portfolio that not only includes furniture, but also interior architecture (walls, floors, etc.), work tools, and technology products. Pathways products are all designed with the same design logic that allows them to work together to deliver a totally integrated work environment with unparalleled changeability. As a result, Pathways' work environments can change as fast as you do—for a lot less. Overall, Pathways delivers a totally new level of integration between architecture, furniture, and technology that makes your work environment a fun place to work and a positive business asset that can have a huge impact on overall business results.

Evaluating Your Company

How does your office environment stack up against the competition? Is it enhancing your recruitment and retention efforts or deterring them? Ask yourself these questions as you reflect on your surroundings:

- Does your office design inhibit or support a team working environment?
- How much time is spent trying to connect with people who are needed to be in the loop?
- How well do your facilities match your values, culture, and image?
- How much freedom are your employees given to request and receive furniture that supports their desired way of working?
- To what degree would employee choice in the selection of their workplace tools or furniture improve productivity and retention?

Best Practices | for Benefits That Keep
Employees Happy, Content,
and Productive

Errand runners and concierge services. Once only re-served for executives, concierge services are now helping overworked employees handle important and time-consuming chores. Accenture (formerly Andersen Consulting) professionals use errand runners who select, wrap, and deliver gifts. One concierge company called HomeRuns delivers groceries to your home and returns rented videos. Employees particularly like services that help them find and make reservations for restaurants and theater. Another favorite among busy employees is assistance with picking up and delivering laundry—a low-tech service providing a high-touch service that moves an employer up one notch on the competition ladder. Companies can expect to pay up to $100 per employee for this service each year.

Employee-sponsored value plans (ESVPs). Businesses are signing up for a new service that provides employee discounts and consumer services in a broad category of areas that can be customized by the employer: auto and home insurance, home equity loans, legal services, credit cards, and discounts at department stores and other retailers. The good news is that this service may cost the employer nothing. For more information, visit <Employeesavings.com> and <you decide.com>.

Job sharing. Job sharing gives employers the brainpower of two people for the cost of one. For those who don't want to work full-time and who value their flexibility and time more than a financial relationship, job sharing is a powerful lure. In general, job sharing works best with such transactional jobs as accounting and customer service, between sharers who have similar communication and work styles, and with those who can work out their own schedules. However, expect management resistance. For more information, see <www.Sharegoals.com>.

Best Practices | for Benefits That Keep
Employees Happy, Content,
and Productive

Time off and sabbaticals. How would you like to go on a
month-long mission trip or take three days to chaperone your
child's school trip and still have a job when you return? Many
businesses are experimenting with allowing employees time
off to prevent burnout and allow additional flexibility in meeting family responsibilities and personal interests. Xerox employees who complete three years of service may take
advantage of the Social Services Leave Program, which per-
mits 8 to 15 employees to work for a nonprofit organization
for 6 to 12 months with full pay and benefits. Large companies are following suit and providing career employees
time to return to college and get additional education.

Paid time off (PTO). Instead of creating separate policies
for sick leave, vacation time, and so on, companies are increasingly looking at PTO to simplify the process. A certain
number of days are lumped or banked into an account for employees to draw from as they please.

Compressed workweeks. A growing number of companies
offer compressed workweeks, which allow people to work
longer hours on fewer days to get an extra day off. Employees
at BP Exploration Inc. in Anchorage, Alaska, may take every
other Friday off. Instantly popular among those who used it,
the option initially caused conflicts when management called
meetings on Fridays. To avoid the problem, BP declared a "no
meetings on Friday" rule. "Compressed workweeks have
helped us handle some pretty rigorous production targets by
giving employees more control and freedom to do the work in
the way that's best for them," says Human Resources Director
Sandy Beitel. "The no-meetings rule offers visible company
support for this arrangement and gives workers some added
comfort about taking that Friday off."

Best Practices | for Benefits That Keep Employees Happy, Content, and Productive

Meditation rooms for employees. Job-related stress is an undeniable part of today's world. According to estimates of the National Safety Council, one million employees are absent on any workday as a result of stress-related issues. Acacia Life Insurance Company in Bethesda, Maryland, and PT & Company in New York City are among the companies offering meditation rooms to lower employee stress. With dim lights, comfortable chairs and couches, and no telephones, these rooms provide a place for employees to get away from it all for a few minutes and return to their work areas refreshed.

Employee-friendly company. Phyliss Brody and Evelyn Greenwald, co-owners of Creativity for Kids, in Cleveland, Ohio, allow some workers to work four-day weeks and take unpaid leave in summer when children are home. In this employee-friendly company, workers say "we" and "our" when speaking about the company and feel free to go to Phyliss and Evelyn with their problems. The owners tell employees when they've done a good job, are willing to hire workers' family members, and provide extra leave to employees with sick children or family members. They even help second-shift workers pay for taxis home. Walls painted sunshine yellow, with photos of employees' children posted everywhere, emphasize the friendly working environment.

Wash your clothes. Wilton Connor Packaging of Charlotte, North Carolina, offers employees some unusual benefits at a modest cost: two laundresses each shift who wash, dry, and fold employees' family laundry while they work; a handyman who makes repairs at workers' houses; and vans to transport workers to and from work, including stops at day care centers.

Best Practices | for Benefits That Keep Employees Happy, Content, and Productive

Lunch as a family. Freddie Mac, a mortgage concern in McLean, Virginia, added baby high chairs and booster seats so that workers could have their babies and young children with them at lunchtime.

Small business involvement techniques. Tom Fouts of Tom Rents, located in Missouri, involves his managers and his hourly workers in making important decisions. Tom's philosophy is more heads are better than one. His employees help decide what items of equipment they should buy. He allows his employees to use any rental equipment they want for their personal use. To improve his benefit package, he recently leased his employees to Simplified Employee Services, which has taken over the administrative management of his employees. Through employee leasing, he can provide an affordable insurance program and other benefits that were previously unaffordable to his small business.

Photos on the wall. TD Industries in Dallas, Texas, makes its employees feel valued, involved, and absolutely equal. One wall in the company has the photographs of all employees who have been with the company more than five years. This "equality" program goes beyond the typical slogans, posters, and HR policies. There are no reserved parking spaces for executives. Everyone uses the same bathrooms and the same water fountains. Everyone is an equal. Maybe that's why TD Industries was listed in 2000 as one of the Top 100 Best Companies by *Fortune* magazine.

Prescription | for Action

- Create a council of employees and management to consider and discuss work-life issues affecting the employees.

- Have managers interview their employees twice a year to consider changes in their work-life arrangements.

- Conduct an internal climate assessment yearly and measure job satisfiers and job dissatisfiers.

- Every six months, meet with all employees to review their benefit programs. Many employees are unaware or fail to take advantage of their benefits.

- Begin the process of becoming an Employer of Choice in your industry.

- Benefits should be printed and distributed to all employees for review every six months.

- Conduct exit interviews to determine the reason people leave your organization.

Chapter Six

Keep the Doorways and Pathways of Communication Open

To improve your workplace environment, what would you like to see your executives/supervisors/managers do?

Sixty-nine percent of the respondents said, "Be better at communicating." *(Chart Your Course Workforce Retention Survey)*

In 1995, the Boeing Company suffered its second-longest walkout ever when the Machinists Union led a 69-day strike against the company. Boeing lost hundreds of millions of dollars and experienced big customer service headaches from missing the delivery dates on 36 airliners.

Part of the problem was that while Boeing "preached" teamwork and productivity, it sent jobs out to lower-cost subcontractors. This disconnect between what management was saying and what it was doing escalated tensions between the union and management.

Boeing's Chairman and President Frank Shrontz blamed the strike on Boeing's "own lack of understanding of worker sentiment and on a failure to communicate corporate concerns to the workforce." Shrontz noted that part of the problem lay with Boeing's "inability to communicate effectively on what we were about and why we were about it."

In 1998 UPS suffered a similar fate when its employees went on strike. UPS lost over $700 million in revenues, suffered a blow to its credibility, and lost the trust of its loyal employees. In retrospect, according to Jerry Frasso, Atlanta human resources director, "No one won." He noted that the walkout could have been prevented had UPS done a better job of communication prior to and during the negotiations.

UPS learned two important lessons from the strike. First, the employees did not fully understand their benefit packages before the strike. Had they understood them, much of the confusion could have been eliminated. The final settlement between the union and management did not significantly increase benefits over the previous contract.

Second, UPS underestimated the need to communicate during the actual negotiation process. To avoid confusing people during the rapidly shifting negotiations, it kept a tight rein on information—a major mistake, as it turned out. Employees wanted to know what was going on, and because they couldn't, many loyal employees felt betrayed by management and walked off the job. The lack of information created a backlash, anger, resentment, legal actions, and lost revenues.

Finally, UPS learned never to assume that your people know what you think they know. When in doubt, overcommunicate!

Information: A collection of facts, content, and data.

Communication: The art and science of delivering thoughts, information, and data to others.

Communication strategy: A system used to ensure that information is delivered to the right people at the right time using the right methodology.

The Importance of Accessibility in Organizations

Good communication is a hallmark of the high-retentionship work environment. At its heart, communication is all about access. In fact, the two basic types of organizations are low-access and high-access.

In a low-access organization, the flow of communication is guarded and restricted—constipated, in fact. People find themselves narrowly confined on the basis of job description, ranking, and location on the organizational chart. It's no surprise that low-access organizations—many of them hierarchical—have greater difficulty responding to change, fluctuating customer needs, and the fluidity of the modern workplace.

In contrast, a high-access organization thrives on information and shares it to the maximum extent possible. The more information people have, the more quickly they can respond to the changing needs of customers and the environment. This doesn't mean that employees must have access to every micron of information available, but they need enough to keep their particular portion of the organization heading in the right direction.

Symptoms of the Low-Access Organization

How do you know if you work in a low-access environment?

- It's a regulatory-based culture, not a people-based culture. A low-access organization is structured around rules, regulations, and policies. Management places more emphasis on enforcing rules than eliminating unnecessary rules and regulations and empowering those closest to the customer.

- Decision making is centralized. The low-access organization has a top-down decision-making process. People on the bottom of the organization put energy into sending good ideas, suggestions, and requests up the chain of command for approval, which is difficult and frustrating. Individual initiative is limited. People wait to be told what to do.

- Mistakes are hard to fix. The low-access organization has a reward system that minimizes change and initiative. Because only the people on the top of the organization are responsible for interpreting and approving any changes to regulations, decision making slows down because the responsibility and power to make decisions is taken away from those who need it the most.

- Change is resisted. A low-access organization protects itself from change. Only a disaster, a threat, or a public relations crisis is enough to initiate change. In the compartmentalized, functionally aligned, department-by-department organization, there is an expert for everything. Different departments don't communicate with each other. People are forced into specialized job descriptions focusing on narrow subject areas.

- The pecking order is defined. In its worst form, a low-access organization becomes a caste system. Top-down layering dictates what roles to take, to whom to talk, and with whom to associate. Rank, position, and educational degrees become more important than results. For innovation and change to exist, people must feel they have equal access to all people, to all levels of the organization.

Which kind of organization has an easier time retaining people? The high-access organization wins hands down.

PeopleSoft: A High-Access Organization

One of the fastest-growing companies in the United States, PeopleSoft grew from 362 employees to 7,500 between 1993 and 1998. Yet even during dizzying growth, it maintained high access and good communication.

One reason is its digital infrastructure, "PeopleBorg," named after the famous Star Trek alien race known for its collective consciousness. PeopleBorg allows everyone access to almost everything within the company, simplifying many of the processes that low-access organizations struggle with. Applicants can access job applications, job descriptions, and all other details and data surrounding the employment process. New hires can use the automated enrollment system to complete all requisite tax forms, schedule an orientation class, pick funds for the 401(k), select employee benefits, and even order business cards. Employees share a Lotus Notes application allowing access to all company projects, technical data, and stages of development.

PeopleSoft employees can also order equipment, design their business cards, and order office supplies directly from their computer. Employees have access to 400 major databases. Almost nothing is off-limits. By allowing all employees access to all this information, the company empowers its employees and facilitates a work environment that is productive and customer focused. This is the type of work environment that young people thrive in. Instant access and high information lead to motivated workers.

PeopleSoft's "infomacracy" offers instant access to everything; no hierarchy gets in the way. People with access have power, and they can't hide behind rules and policies. As PeopleSoft CEO David Duffield says, "We create systems that let people be brilliant rather than push paper."

Creating the High-Access Organization

The larger an organization, the greater the danger it may become rigid and inflexible. Unless it's careful, it will engender a bureaucracy where rules, regulations, policies, procedures, and "I need permission to make a decision" become the norm.

Today's businesses must change course quickly. Communication and information are essential to innovation, high retention, and change. And they have to flow freely. Everyone needs access to important information!

Communication must also be clear. A survey by Office-Team, based in Menlo Park, California, found that 14 percent of each 40-hour workweek is wasted because of poor communication. It's not a simple process, nor is there one ideal way to accomplish good communication. An effective communication strategy takes into consideration how the human brain processes and stores information. Be sure you communicate in ways that have an impact on people on visual, emotional, personal, and analytical levels.

And keep in mind that communication flows two different ways: from the top of the organization down and from the bottom of the organization up. Be sure your strategy includes forms of communication that send information downward to the people who work within the organization as well as forms of communication that allow the people who work within the organization to send information up to those who are leading the organization.

To create a high-access organization, make communication a top priority. Your goal should be to provide the right kinds of information in the right delivery mode to the people who work for you. Match the communication method to the message and the audience who receives it, and use the checklist to plan your high-access communication strategy.

High-Access Communication Checklist

✓ Speak regularly about the vision, mission, and goals of your department and organization.

✓ Hold regular "town meetings" to keep people informed of changes and new information.

✓ Your plans should include all people in the organization—from the lowest to the highest.

✓ Include all telecommuters, distance-based and part-time people, and volunteers in communication efforts.

✓ Initiate procedures to ensure supervisors distribute information down to their staff.

✓ Conduct employee surveys to sample attitudes and opinions.

✓ Identify what information is critical to the success and morale of the staff.

✓ Hold managers accountable for communicating to their employees.

✓ People will interpret your message and intent differently, so consider cultural differences and adapt accordingly.

✓ Once is not enough. Communicate your message in multiple formats.

What People Need to Know

Many business leaders "protect" their employees from what is happening outside their four walls. But it's management's job to look beyond the horizon and prepare for the future. Protecting employees from reality only makes people oblivious to the changes and perils raging just outside their walls. When tragedy strikes, fear, blame, and mistrust destroy the cocoon and swallow everyone.

High-retention businesses can't afford to protect their employees from reality. Keep everyone informed. Pass along everything you can about

- success stories,
- targets,
- goals,
- good news and bad news,
- long-term plans,
- short-term plans,
- company difficulties,
- new products and services,
- concerns about the future,
- customer expectations/problems,
- what competitors are doing,
- updates on benefits,
- shortfalls,
- where to focus time and energy,
- eliminating rumors, and
- technological advances impacting the organization.

Tools and Techniques That Create High Access and High Retention

Bobcat of Kentucky, a construction equipment company located in Louisville, Kentucky, provides high access to all of its employees. According to former owner Rodger McAlister, turnover is almost nonexistent—quite an accomplishment in an industry that is 80,000 technicians short.

Although part of Bobcat's success is due to its generous profit-sharing plan, in which employees and service technicians can receive up to $700,000 upon retirement, Rodger's open-book approach to communication and management also gets credit.

Rodger says a lot of businesses practice "mushroom management"—they keep their employees in the dark and feed them fertilizer—but Rodger's approach is the opposite. Every day, employees are given all the sales figures for the year to date, right up to the previous day. On Fridays, everyone rotates jobs for one hour. A parts person becomes a service technician and vice versa. These high-access techniques build a stronger team, improve communication within the company, and capture new ideas for running the business.

High-access companies that are committed to open communication can avail themselves of a host of tools and techniques. Let's take a look at some.

Personal Communication

The relationship between the individual and his or her supervisor is a key factor causing people to stay or to go. All supervisors must be able to relate to others in a positive and productive manner.

Nothing is more powerful than a simple conversation between two people. In today's fast-moving organizations, interpersonal contact is an ever more important ingredient in employee retention.

Make a priority of spending time talking and listening to people. No agenda needed—it doesn't even have to be about work. Talk about the employee's family, pets, hobbies—whatever matters most.

Invest time in learning to provide and receive feedback. At Southeastern Container Inc., new team members go off-site and out to breakfast with the general manger, HR director, and fellow team members, thus providing an opportunity for new people to share and provide feedback on their feelings about the orientation, the training, and the company in general.

The Human Resources Department of Nations Healthcare Inc. initiated a "Breakfast with the President" program to improve communications between employees and the CEO. Each breakfast begins with coffee and biscuits and ends when the discussion ends. Results: higher morale and a sense of "openness."

At BellSouth in Atlanta, the CIO meets once a month with employees to share the results of the previous quarter. He also shares current issues and addresses rumors. He takes questions from employees placed on three-by-five-inch cards and provides immediate feedback. This process keeps the lines of communication open between all levels of the organization.

Many managers mistakenly think they are good communicators. If you're unsure of your ability to communicate with your employees, begin to upgrade your interpersonal skills today. Nothing replaces the interpersonal dynamic of one-to-one communication; no skill is more important when it comes to building a high-retention culture. Yet too many people are uncertain of their interpersonal abilities. In an *Investors Business Daily* poll that used a scale from 1 to 10, only half of the executives polled gave themselves a rating of 8 to 10. If you feel your skills merit a 7 or lower, develop a plan for improving them.

Storytelling

The art of storytelling existed before books, computers, and e-mail. Telling stories and using personal illustrations are powerful and effective tools to communicate ideas and information, particularly when people are experiencing information overload. A story can cut through clutter and make the abstract clear and concrete.

Storytelling crosses all boundaries, cultures, backgrounds, and company positions. Communicating through personal illustrations and stories takes more time but is a more effective way to provide important information and relate to people on a personal level.

Horst Shultze, CEO of Ritz-Carlton Hotels, is one of the best speakers I have heard. His secret: using stories to illustrate his talks. I've heard him tell how, when he left home as a young boy to work in the hotel industry, his grandfather tried to discourage him by telling him he needed to get a "real job." He used that tale as a springboard to describe his dream of creating not just good hotels but the best hotel chain in the world.

Listening to Shultze is transforming. He doesn't read a prepared text written by some speechwriter but speaks from his heart. When I heard him, you could feel his commitment and caring. It wasn't the words he used but the tone of his words and his body language that made the difference.

Through storytelling, Shultze's listeners can tell that he has earned the right and the credibility to be the CEO of his company.

Storytelling Topics

- Legendary examples of great achievers
- Personal examples of mistakes made
- Self-deprecating humor
- Top performers from the company
- Personal triumphs over tragedy
- Personal goals
- What the "enemy," or competition, is doing

Newsletters

A well-designed and well-written newsletter can turn a cold, impersonal workplace into a warmer, friendlier, and more people-oriented place of business. It can be a valuable tool for improving morale and motivation and for communicating important information in a nonthreatening manner.

People like to read newsletters, particularly if they include information about the people who work in the organization. They provide an excellent platform to acknowledge promotions, awards, and recognition and provide important milestones in employees' personal lives. People want to see plenty of pictures and articles about

- successes of coworkers;
- staff changes and promotions;
- personal news such as births, marriages, birthdays, and anniversaries;
- employees and/or their family members;
- personal interest stories;
- volunteer work;
- company vision, mission, and goals;
- job-related "how-to" information;
- benefits;
- financial results;
- tips to improve productivity;
- survey data; and
- contest winners.

Jeff Rubin, a newsletter specialist who owns *Put It in Writing* in Pinole, California, believes that the proliferation of e-mail and the Internet has caused professionally published newsletters to increase in value. Like many professional writers, he recommends that companies invest in a quality product. If you do a newsletter, make sure it is done well. A professionally published newsletter should

- be easy to read, in just one sitting;
- have lots of content and avoid generic cut-and-paste filler material;
- include "how-to" information to energize and educate readers;
- reflect the attitude and personality of the organization;
- be published consistently—monthly, quarterly, or yearly— and stick to a schedule;
- focus less on company politics and more on employee needs;
- use plain language, avoiding industry jargon and current business buzzwords that may not be meaningful to everyone in the company.

Town Hall Meetings

Town hall meetings can give workers access to management and let management convey important news to employees. Open to anyone who wants to attend, they can be used to disperse important information affecting everyone within the organization. Don't forget to include family members, partners, and other employee support groups in the process.

Focus Groups and Sensing Sessions

These tools will help you find out how people feel about a particular issue and generate specific answers to specific issues. An outside facilitator may be appropriate when employees are asked to speak about internal issues. Workers in traditionally structured organizations are more willing to speak to an outsider than to someone from within the organization. Make sure you don't use just any outsider; use a trained consultant or facilitator.

Employee Hot Lines

Providing employees a phone line to call for information improves bottom-up communication. Anyone can call to vent problems, ask questions, or get information. The service can be expanded to 24 hours a day by adding voice mail or a recorder. Make sure, however, that you get back to the employee in a timely manner, or you may do more harm than good and damage credibility.

Props

In 1997 Lawrence Weinbach was hired to help Unisys transform itself from a mainframe computer maker into a service provider—no easy task! During the difficult transition, Weinbach kept his message simple and understandable, and focused on three key points: reputation, customers, and employees. To illustrate the three points, he repeated, "If one of the legs is broken, you can't sit on the stool." On his suit he wore a tiny gold stool symbolizing his message. As he visited and spoke with over 12,000 employees, his message of transformation gradually took hold, and one Christmas he received six three-legged stools and a sweatshirt that said, "We believe."

Thanks to Weinbach's commitment, Unisys made the transformation from mainframe manufacturer to customer service provider, and its share of services doubled and have been growing consistently ever since.

Signed, *Anonymous*

Employees with complaints about their work often choose to voice their unhappiness via an anonymous letter to the chief executive. Often ignored in the past, today executives see such letters as a source of possibly important information.

George Fisher, chairman and CEO of the Eastman Kodak Company, gives his e-mail address to everyone and receives unsigned messages every week. Multiple complaints about the same situation receive special attention based on the "where there's smoke, there's fire" attitude.

At Browning-Ferris Industries, Inc., employees submit unsigned complaints via an open electronic forum that disguises the identity of the writer. Replies are posted each day on an electronic bulletin board. Messages are screened for slander or redundancy before being posted.

Rite Aid Corporation decided to encourage employee input after acquiring Thrifty Payless Holdings Inc. It installed an outside voice mail service so former Thrifty Payless employees could leave messages at any time. The service prepares verbatim transcripts for clients, thereby protecting the identity of the callers.

One word of caution: unsigned complaints may possibly open the door to future litigation because the company received notice of a problem. They also involve the risk of hurting someone's reputation and/or spreading misinformation. It can also be difficult for managers to respond without sufficient specific information.

Don't Confuse Technology with Communication

You'd think that with so many ways to communicate—cell phones, the Internet, e-mail, personal digital assistants, pagers, and so on—our ability to communicate would improve. But the opposite seems to be true: as technology advances, the quality of communication declines. Put another way, as the quantity of communication tools increases, the quality of communication decreases. People are reaching a saturation level— what I call *technosaturation syndrome.*

Technology has a voracious appetite. The time it takes to program, service, feed, and then read the data streaming from all those LCD panels makes people's lives hectic and stressful and blurs the distinction between valuable information and noise.

More technology creates a need for a more personal approach, a return to more traditional, "high-touch" approaches to communication. As I have stressed, people want the right kind of information, and they want it delivered on a more personal level.

That said, it's true that voice mail, e-mail, speakerphones, and cellular/portable phones are all standard parts of the modern business world. Unfortunately, easier and faster do not always mean better or acceptable—even if "everybody else does it." Common sense and courtesy are still important communication ingredients.

Avoid anger in your communications.   Expressing anger is a big temptation when speaking to a machine or dashing out a message on your computer keyboard because you are not face-to-face with the other person. A knee-jerk message could be very offensive. Later, but too late, you may wish you could take back angry words on someone's voice mail or a sarcastic e-mail message. The answering machine or computer will not respond to your angry message—but the recipient probably will!

E-mail

One of the problems with e-mail is that it can make an important message seem informal and unimportant, especially when the recipient is swamped with e-mail messages. A message's urgency and personal touch are lost in the blizzard.

E-mail is still business correspondence, so keep it business-like. Basic points: Include a subject line; do not use uppercase for all letters (it's harder to read and comes across as yelling at the reader); check your grammar and spelling because they reflect on you, even in e-mail; and sign off with your name, company name (if applicable), and a phone number.

If your e-mail is a reply, even though the subject line will provide a general reference, include enough information to ensure the recipient can quickly identify the reply. It is not always necessary to include the entire original message in your answer.

Don't be upset if you do not receive an answer immediately. People have other responsibilities besides reading e-mail. If you require an immediate response, it may be best to simply pick up the telephone and call the person.

Answering Machines and Voice Mail

Record the outgoing message in your own voice. Keep it short and businesslike. The caller assumes you're sorry you missed his or her call without being told. Do not include comments of a religious nature, and stay away from such clichés as "Have a nice day." Make the day nice for your callers with a brief message in a pleasant tone.

When you leave a message, don't assume the caller will recognize your voice. State your name and, if appropriate, your company name. Some systems automatically record date/time information, but you may want to state that also if you feel it is important. Keep your message brief. Speak clearly and slowly when you give your phone number. Someone who has to listen to your message six times in order to understand the number may not care whether he or she returns your call.

Speakerphones

Love to use your speakerphone? Courtesy dictates that you ask the caller for permission before you activate the speaker function. Also, remember that everyone within hearing distance may hear the conversation whether or not they should.

If you use a speakerphone to conduct a meeting, introduce everyone present because the person on the other end of the line cannot see who is in the room. This is good manners and can help avoid embarrassing situations. The caller may wish to monitor his or her comments according to who is present.

Best Practices | for Creating High Access

Ten-minute meetings. Some Japanese companies practice *Chorei* staff meetings each morning. These ten-minute meetings at which employees stand up—no chairs allowed—provide a strong beginning for the day. They worked for Caterpillar and Mitsubishi when they jointly developed a hydraulic shovel.

Blank agenda. For a more productive meeting with more staff participation, post a blank meeting agenda in the employee area. Employees jot down questions and/or issues for staff meetings. You'll also discover many practical topics and concerns you weren't aware of previously.

Stuff the staff meeting. Bob Felton, a former navy commander and now president of software developer Indus Group, eliminated all routine staff meetings because he felt they had become a time-wasting venture. Now, meetings are held only when really needed.

Hold "skip-level" meetings. Skip-level meetings mix hourly and salaried employees with management to generate a pleasing mix of ideas. Providing either pizza or donuts always makes them better meetings.

Share and learn. BellSouth Advertising & Publishing holds monthly or quarterly meetings where a representative of one department gives a 20- to 30-minute presentation on the work of his or her department. Employees also discuss how what each department/team does impacts the other.

A day without meetings! Certain departments at the *Atlanta Journal-Constitution* have meeting-free Fridays.

Keep it light. Meetings go better if you use rooms with lots of natural light, which tells the brain to produce serotonin. Serotonin induces people to be awake and alert, so stay away from meeting rooms with muted light.

Best Practices | for Creating High Access

Share the news. The Bethany Care Society shares staff members' successes and ideas through a bimonthly newsletter attached to the pay stubs of every employee.

The union wins. Union leaders with the Hawaii State Teachers Association recognize members of management who are outstanding leaders, thus improving communication and building trust between union and management.

Anonymous suggestions/question box. Fortis Financial Group uses suggestion boxes for people to ask questions they don't feel comfortable asking in person. Management addresses the questions in a monthly newsletter.

Fast food, fast information. Applebee's "Hey, Lloyd" program lets employees send a note straight to CEO Lloyd Hill. Its Appleseed program lets employees test unconventional ideas, policies, and procedures in two restaurants in Kansas City. And its policy of requiring all corporate office people to pull a shift in a local restaurant each year builds access. Even CEO Hill has pulled his shift as a busboy.

Cellular/Portable Phones

When you accept an incoming call while with another person, realize that other person may not appreciate the interruption. A client especially may feel in a position of "second place" in such a situation. Also, when you conduct business within hearing distance of other people, someone may overhear information not meant for their ears. Last but not least, be careful of what you say—someone with more curiosity than manners or ethics may tap in and listen.

Prescription | for Action

- Consider training people to understand the differences in communication across cultures.

- Create a formalized plan to spread information throughout the organization.

- Assign someone within the organization with the sole responsibility of managing information. Consider creating a position of director of internal communications or information.

- Spend a portion of time just walking around and talking to people.

- Don't hide bad news. Be up front. Rumors thrive when workers aren't kept informed.

- Urge people to learn how to use the company intranet, the Internet, and other company-provided communication technologies.

- Don't rely on e-mail to deliver important messages.

- Make time to talk to people on an informal basis.

Chapter Seven

Create a Charged Work Environment That Energizes and Engages

Southern Company CEO A. W. "Bill" Dahlberg believes in having fun. At company gatherings, he has impersonated soul singer James Brown . . . dressed as General George Patton . . . and arrived decked out as a fortune-teller complete with crystal ball.

Employees at PeopleSoft, Inc., remember the day that CEO David Duffield danced the macarena in front of 500 happy coworkers.

Over at Odetics, Inc., they're still talking about the time the chief technology officer took over duty on the cafeteria cash register on St. Patrick's Day . . . dressed as a leprechaun!

And then there's John Briggs, director of production at Yahoo!. In early 1997, Briggs promised salespeople that he would have the Web directory's logo tattooed on his posterior when the stock passed $50 a share. To show he had kept his promise, he modeled the new tattoo in front of everyone in the company.

Finally, there's Disney. Years ago, I was sitting on a bus just outside Walt Disney World's recycling center listening to the driver explain how trash from Disney World is brought here, transformed into fertilizer, and then sterilized, sealed in bags, and sold to farmers. When a big pile of freshly sterilized fertilizer came flowing out of a chute, the excited bus driver told me about the contest to name this fertilizer. Looking me straight in the eye, he asked me to guess what the cast members wanted to name the fertilizer.

Zippity Doo Doo.

Energize: To give energy; to invigorate; to supply with electric current. *Engage:* To attract and hold.

"To improve your workplace environment, what would you like to see your executives/supervisors/managers do?"

Thirty-six percent said, "Try new things at work." Twenty-six percent said, "Be more fun" *(Chart Your Course Workforce Retention Survey)*

One thing that has held steady throughout my career— from my days of working on the Apollo program to my days of developing cars at Ford—is that in any successful innovation, there is one magic ingredient: a strong, motivating goal that everyone on a team can easily understand and embrace. (William Powers, vice president–research, Ford Motor Company)

Engage and Energize Your Workforce

After a lifetime identifying what it takes to transform ordinary organizations into high-retention organizations, I know that work can be awfully boring—unless someone at the top shakes everything up!

The extraordinary leaders and organizations I just mentioned know that in order to engage and energize people about their work, you need to lighten up and have some fun every now and then. It isn't hard to dress up as a leprechaun, sponsor a company contest, or throw a party. And the payoff for an energized work environment is enormous: improved retention and productivity and reduced turnover.

As Chapter 3 made clear, we can't merely employ someone's hands and tell them to leave their hearts, minds, and spirits at home. Today's workers are looking for many things in an employment relationship. They want a meaningful partnership with their workplaces. Workplaces that provide meaning and purpose *and* are fun, engaging, and energizing will enjoy greater retention, higher productivity, and lower turnover.

Remember Abraham Maslow? His well-known hierarchy of needs theory posited that all people strive for self-actualization, which is the need for innovation and creativity. When people can reach this higher level on the job, they gain greater personal fulfillment, which improves job satisfaction. Yes, you still have to pay well, but an organization that can create an energized, "higher calling" environment will have higher retention and greater productivity.

Jobs and work environments that use high-involvement activities provide people with autonomy, learning opportunities, meaning, purpose, and a way to grow and get ahead—not to mention providing a host of benefits to the company as well. High-involvement activities include, but are not limited to, the use of self-managing teams, information sharing, shared goal setting, flexible work hours, suggestion programs, brainstorming sessions, Kaizen, idea campaigns, and motivational meetings.

Advantages Gained for Using High-Involvement Activities

Advantages for the Company	*Advantages for the Employee*
Higher retention	Positive feelings of self-worth
Improved communications	Reward and recognition
Quicker response to a changing environment	
	Improved motivation
Less resistance to change	Professional development
Cost cutting	Pride in one's job
Improved processes and systems	Greater loyalty
Continuous improvement	Greater flexibility
Increased profits	Freedom and autonomy
Higher motivation	Fun
Higher levels of customer service	Personal fulfillment
Better products and services	

Figure 7.1 Positive Impact of High-Involvement Activities on
Organizational Performance

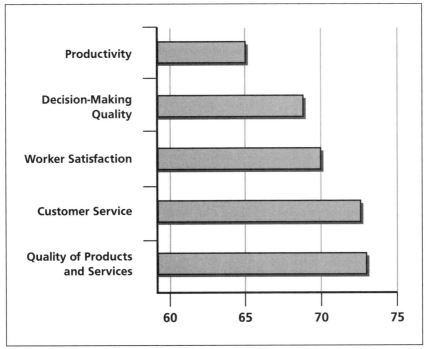

These benefits were confirmed by a survey conducted by Development Dimensions International (DDI), which asked 232 organizations around the world (including 81 from Hong Kong, Thailand, the Philippines, Singapore, and Indonesia) to answer the question, "Do high-performance practices improve business performance and which practices have the greatest impact?"

The findings from the survey showed significant improvements in all five areas, as Figure 7.1 indicates. Most noteworthy were the improvements in the areas of customer service and quality of the products and services. Furthermore, I would be so bold as to estimate that the biggest changes were not measured directly but more implicitly. Although the survey did not measure the improvement of attitudes, retention rates, and feelings of the workforce, I'm sure they improved. As Abraham Maslow indicated in his theory of motivation, the more ability and freedom people have to use their thinking ability, the more satisfaction they receive on the job and the higher they move up the pyramid of needs. People do not respond favorably to overly restrictive work environments. High-involvement activities help people reach higher levels.

Creating the Right Spirit

The easiest way to create and implement an energized work environment is to remember the word *spirit:*

S—Set a motivating goal or target that shapes the environment and gives people purpose and direction.

P—Provide a process to capture people's ideas.

I—Ideas count.

R—Results motivate people.

I—Involve elements of fun, enthusiasm, surprise, and timing.

T—Teams build on the efforts of others.

Let's look at how each step works.

Set a Motivating Goal or Target That Shapes the Environment and Gives People a Purpose and Direction

Years ago a man named Billy Payne attracted a lot of attention by setting a goal most thought was improbable: to bring the Centennial Olympic games to Atlanta, Georgia. When this goal became a reality, a lightning bolt of energy shot through all who became part of the 1996 Olympics. That attraction and energy persuaded me to become an Olympic volunteer. I knew it was a once-in-a-lifetime opportunity: my chance to be part of something bigger than myself.

Listening to the radio and driving downtown on my first day as VIP driver assigned to shuttle dignitaries around Atlanta, I heard about the Olympic Park bombing. As the announcer talked about the dead and injured, I was dazed, incredulous, and almost in shock. I grew angry at the thought that this bomber killed and hurt innocent people—even angrier realizing that someone tried to damage and maybe put an end to all we had worked for. I was certain the bombing would dampen the enthusiasm we volunteers were feeling. I just knew that my coworkers were going to stay home for their own protection. I asked myself, "Who in their right mind would volunteer to put their life in harm's way?"

Amazingly, everyone showed up for work—and more determined than ever. They were not about to let this event damage the Olympic spirit, let alone stop them from fulfilling their jobs.

If Atlanta's Olympic volunteers were willing to give thousands of hours of their time even in the face of threatening circumstances, can't we generate a proportional amount of energy, passion, and purpose at work?

Olympic Performance Events and Big Hairy Goals

Every organization has a pulse: fast, slow, or, in some sad instances, nonexistent. Attach an EKG to a person or (if you could) to an organization, and you discover the same thing: the heart rate adapts to circumstances by accelerating or decelerating. When work is routine—filling out reports, answering e-mail, attending meetings—the heart rate is calm and quiet. Although these activities are important, they don't require a higher level of thinking and ability and can become boring. Too much routine can make even the most committed employee lose interest in his or her work.

It's analogous to the lives of firefighters. They spend most of their time handling routine maintenance, training, and safety inspections. But that routine prepares them for the few moments they spend fighting fires or responding to emergencies. The emergency engages them and calls upon all their resources, creating a heightened level of awareness that results in heroic actions and superhuman levels of performance.

Like firefighters, our heart rates spike in circumstances that are physical, dangerous, or stimulating. Likewise, performance levels soar when people are stimulated. To create an energy spike in an organization, I recommend launching an Olympic Performance Event (OPE).

An Olympic Performance Event creates a temporary period of time that stimulates people to reach a higher state of performance and/or creativity. OPEs have several benefits:

- They energize people, allowing them to experience purpose and passion.
- They give people a feeling of expectation and excitement.
- They drive a higher level of thinking.
- They raise creativity and innovation.
- They give people a feeling of accomplishment.
- They break up the routine of work.

Of course, people cannot perform at Olympic levels all the time. If they try, eventually they will burn out—or end up physically incapacitated in a hospital or a funeral home. Don't try to run an OPE every week. Some work simply must be routine. It's normal, acceptable, and vital to most organizations. The key is to break up the monotony and give people something to talk about—a goal they can conquer.

On Fun Friday, employees of the Dallas unit of Sprint Corporation enjoy novel experiences like swapping plants or attending ice cream socials served by managers wearing aprons. Employees of Nike in Beaverton, Oregon, can't wait for Thursday to roll around. They stop work at 4:30 in the afternoon, savor some beer and soda, and then kayak across a lake, race bikes, and compete in a 600-yard run.

Tradition calls for employees at the Hyatt Regency in Lexington, Kentucky, to wrap a 12-pound frozen turkey with electrical tape, roll it 50 feet down the loading dock (toward the human resources office!), and try to turn over as many wine bottle "bowling pins" as possible. Winners get a pumpkin pie.

In their book *Visionary Leadership,* James C. Collins and Jerry Porras have a similar concept called "Big Hairy Audacious Goals" (BHAGs). They talk about how important it is for leaders to create these goals to engage people and to stimulate progress. Whether you call a goal or an event an OPE or a BHAG, the point is to get people excited and energized about work.

Provide a Process to Capture People's Ideas

Once an environment has been energized, an organization needs a way to capture the energy and ideas that start churning. Focus groups, idea campaigns, motivational meetings, and implementation teams are among the techniques common today.

Key Elements of a Successful Idea Program
- Top management support and involvement
- Communication
- Element of surprise: Teaser Week
- Idea coordinators
- Implementation team
- Fun
- Reward and recognition

Idea programs offer many advantages. For starters, they improve individual motivation and morale of the workforce. They also allow departments and individuals to work cross-functionally and create an environment of learning and constant renewal. They improve work methods and processes continually, reduce the costs of doing business, improve safety, and reduce accidents. Exchanging ideas always improves communication within an organization, and the knowledge that top management is open to, and will act on, the ideas of all reduces the we/ they syndrome.

Good Idea Boards

Georgia's Buckhead Ritz-Carlton Hotel has a unique way to capture ideas and promote continuous improvement from front-line workers. Employees write their ideas on an easy-wipe board in their department. Instead of passing untested ideas up the chain of command, the employee who originates an idea has the responsibility for its achievement. Employees follow a three-step work process: study it, pilot it, and adopt it.

A quality coach helps each department and its employees with the process. Once an idea is piloted and found worthwhile, it is adopted. Each month the department forwards the best idea to the division and then on to the Quality Office for special recognition. The department awards $10 for the best idea of the month. The best idea of the division gets $50 or brunch in the hotel's restaurant. At the hotel level, the best idea receives $100 or dinner for two. In addition, the winners receive letters of appreciation and an invitation to a quarterly reception courtesy of the Ritz-Carlton Hotel.

Ideas don't have to be big to be good. One innovative door attendant had the idea to pipe music into the first floor restroom. He talked to the engineering department director to see how hard it would be to implement. He and the engineering director went to the restroom, and found speakers and wires already in place. All they had to do was connect the wires, flip a switch, and the idea came to life!

Idea Campaigns

Most suggestion programs fail. Suggestion boxes sit and collect dust, and approved suggestions are few and far between.

Getting employees' ideas and getting their involvement is critical in our rapidly changing world. If your company is going to be competitive, it's mandatory to involve not just hands but also minds and ideas from everyone in your organization.

An effective approach to the suggestion program is the idea campaign. Over and done with in four weeks, this month-long campaign can generate hundreds of ideas on improving productivity and motivation and cutting costs.

The goal is to get at least one idea from everyone in the organization. For the first idea, each person receives a coffee cup. A second idea is acknowledged with a writing pen or a rubber buck. At the end of each week, a special award ceremony recognizes everyone who turned in ideas or suggestions. Names drawn from a basket receive other prizes and gifts.

Because the program only lasts three to four weeks, the program generates a tremendous amount of focused energy and motivation. No one wants to be left out of the program—everyone participates. All ideas have to be considered and all suggesters receive instantaneous recognition. For participants, the most powerful force is not the awards but the feeling that management is listening to their ideas. More detailed information on this program is provided at our Web site <www.chartcourse.com>.

Mini-Kaizens

Many U.S. companies and many Japanese companies use *Kaizen,* which means "continuous improvement." Kaizen processes are found mostly in manufacturing environments, but a Mini-Kaizen (MK), the smaller brother, is appropriate for all organizations seeking ways to engage employees and their ideas.

A Mini-Kaizen is tightly managed and operates on a compressed schedule. The goal is to finish in one day or less. An MK can be used to map out an administrative process, design a retention plan, or create a customer service strategy. An outside facilitator who is familiar with the MK process is the key to success. The outline for a day's event is as follows:

- Conduct team training—2 hours
- Define the purpose/mission statement—30 minutes
- Identify and map out present system, if any—1 hour
- Brainstorm areas of improvement—1 hour
- Map out a new process—45 minutes
- Delegate responsibility and implement changes—1 hour
- Presentation to management—15 minutes

To prevent the meeting from becoming laborious or contentious, members are not allowed to talk during some parts of the brainstorming sessions called "Silent Sorts." Members stand up and move around a lot, which minimizes boredom. At the conclusion, the organization has an implementation plan and everyone owns the design, which speeds up the implementation process.

Idea Expositions

The Sony Corporation is well known for its ability to create and manufacture new and innovative products. Each year Sony generates approximately 1,000 new products and product innovations. Founder Masaru Ibuka's philosophy for success is "never follow others."

To foster the exchange of ideas within departments, Sony's Corporate Research sponsors an annual Idea Exposition. During the exposition, scientists and engineers display projects and ideas they are working on. Open only to Sony's employees, the exposition lets individuals share ideas otherwise protected by departmental walls. This process creates a healthy climate of innovation and creativity at all levels of the organization.

Ideas Count

The best way to deenergize people is to ask for their ideas and then ignore them.

It's far better not to ask for ideas than it is to ask and then fail to do anything with them. People cherish their ideas like their children. Even though not all ideas are usable, it is essential for a manager to nurture all new ideas and the people who provide them. The idea represents the spirit and soul of those individuals!

Unfortunately, bureaucracy always kills ideas. A traditional, hierarchical organization restricts the free-flowing give and take of ideas and makes their exchange difficult. The system becomes more important and protects itself from individual initiative and innovation. Fewer ideas are volunteered, and many of those are screened, set aside, or ignored by management. When people hear no too many times, they stop volunteering new ideas.

Once you energize your organization and set up a process for collecting new ideas, you need to make sure that someone is listening—and that the answer to a new proposal is yes.

The words, body language, and facial expressions we use all reveal if we value the idea or not. Manage ideas using the SWARM process.

- **S:** Suspend judgment. When you first hear a new idea, don't judge it. Seize its intent. Avoid speaking negatively and damaging the suggester's ego. All ideas are greater in scope than we first hear.
- **W:** Watch for connections. See how the idea relates to other ideas you have heard or problems you need to solve.
- **A:** Adjust your thinking to the possibilities the idea possesses.
- **R:** Recognize the suggester and encourage him or her to submit more ideas.

- **M:** Make it happen. Once you grasp the idea, take action. Let the person know why (or why not) or how and when the idea will go into effect. Above all, *don't* form a committee to study the idea, ask the individual to develop a complete action plan, or pass the idea off to someone else to evaluate.

Results Motivate People

Engagement and energy come when people see the results of their ideas.

Sometimes people are reluctant to act on the ideas of others. A successful idea program must consider and act on ideas quickly. To motivate managers to evaluate and decide on suggestions and ideas more rapidly, Parker Bertea, a division of Parker Hannifin, selected two evaluators and called them its "top guns." To add special prestige to this new role, it gave them "fighter ace style hats" and then placed their pictures on the bulletin board so all knew who was reviewing the ideas. As a result, managers went from six months to two months to implement a new idea.

Raychem celebrates stealing other departments' ideas and applying them to a job. "Stealers" get certificates that say, "I stole somebody else's idea, and I'm using it." The person who had the original idea also gets an award and a certificate saying, "I had a great idea, and so-and-so is using it."

Ron Eardley, executive vice president of Image National, used employee input to help salvage the failing commercial sign designer and manufacturer. At off-site meetings, he had all 77 employees review financial information, safety procedures, and quality issues. He used employee-initiated teams to tackle problems; one project saved an estimated $40,000. Involving employees in the decision-making process also lowered turnover.

Involve Elements of FEST: *F*un, *E*nthusiasm, *S*urprise, and *T*iming

The old saying "Crazy like a fox" may apply to what some executives are doing to energize their employees. Remember Bill Dahlberg, who has dressed as James Brown and General George Patton? David Duffield, who danced the macarena? And John Briggs, who displayed his tattoo after he lost his bet? These executives are breaking the monotony of work and the status quo by setting an example at the top.

Bill Dahlberg's Atlanta office includes baseball caps, a nun puppet that can throw a punch, stuffed animals, and gloves that make motorcycle sounds. Dahlberg keeps the items around to remind him there's a world outside his office with people who care what they're doing.

When he isn't dancing the macarena, PeopleSoft CEO David Duffield is answering his own phone and opening his own mail in his own cubicle. Annual employee turnover is 3 percent, or one-quarter of the national average. Employees who earn outstanding service awards get either $500 in cash or 100 stock options.

Hal Rosenbluth, CEO of Rosenbluth International, one of the nation's largest travel services company, believes in creating a fun work environment. He starts by hiring "nice people," because he believes nice people like to work together and like to have fun. Officers dedicate every Tuesday afternoon to serving high tea and discussing corporate values with new recruits at the company's Philadelphia headquarters. Any associate can contact Rosenbluth on a special toll-free 800 number. To get feedback on the company, he uses a sort of Crayola Rorschach test, in which associates are sent crayons and blank paper and asked to render their view of the company. A "happiness barometer" team meets every six months to benchmark attitudes and enjoyment levels.

Joel Slutzky, cofounder of Odetics Inc., a company that makes robots and spacecraft flight recorders, uses "structured spontaneity" to enliven his company. (It was his chief technology officer who appeared at the cafeteria cash register one St. Patrick's Day dressed as a leprechaun.) Managers also allow associates to cover the hallways with maps and photographs of their hometowns.

Herb Kelleher, CEO and founder of Southwest Airlines, combines fun and hard work into something he calls "management by fooling around." At the nonconformist airline, everything demonstrates that something is different—from the tickets and boarding passes to the casual dress and occasional costumes attendants wear.

An important part of Southwest's culture is the requirement that one day each quarter, all managers work at a different front-line job to help them learn more about the company. They have served as luggage handlers, gate agents, and flight attendants. Even Kelleher has helped load luggage onto the planes. Kelleher wants his executives to be guiding examples. He also feels that everyone is a leader and has attempted to limit rules and regulations so that people can make decisions at the lowest possible level. Kelleher says, "We tell our people that we value inconsistency."

CEO Robert Shillman of Cognex, a Boston software company, welcomes new employees with a Three Stooges routine. Workers, known as "Cognoids," refer to Shillman as "Dr. Bob." The dozens of stunts he's dreamed up include leading them in a corporate anthem accompanied by an employee rock band, tossing moneybags with cash bonuses up to $10,000 out of a Brink's truck, and rewarding 15-year veterans with trips to one of the Seven Wonders of the World. Shillman believes his efforts help break down barriers between management and workers.

Former Campbell Soup CEO David W. Johnson arrived in January 1990 accompanied by trumpets sounding, "Mmmm, Mmmm, Good." The CEO once donned a red cape and called himself "Souperman, Top Spoon" and on another occasion led a rally in a jockey's outfit. Johnson communicates his strategy and aligns his troops behind his vision, while backing his cheerleading with iron discipline.

Teams Build on the Efforts of Others

The advantages of using workplace teams for team-building cannot be overemphasized in creating the high-retention work environment. In a rapidly changing world that values high technology, speed, and flexibility, teams provide a key ingredient for success.

People place major importance in the relationships with their coworkers. In fact, the relationships with their coworkers rank higher than the actual relationship with the employer.

At the beginning of each quarterly associates meeting, Professional Data, a software development company, practices something called "enthusiastic starts." The president chooses five or six individuals from one department to present the enthusiastic start. The meetings usually start around 7:30 in the morning, so it's meant to be an "eye opener" that wakes everyone up. And it usually succeeds.

One team rewrote the YMCA song to fit the company. The group dressed like the Village People and danced as they sang. Another group wrote a skit based on the television program *Brady Bunch,* using computer software to portray the family in blocks as seen on the beginning of the show. Another skit based on *Star Wars* portrayed the company's competitors as the "dark side."

Best Practices | for Creating a Charged Work Environment

Celebrate holidays. At one company, the sales director puts on a costume mask and walks around all the departments a few days before Halloween. In another, all the managers dress up in costumes and give away candy to all the employees. And every company has someone who looks just like Santa!

Mission Impossible Award. First American honors individuals who can solve tough problems with unique awards: the Mission Impossible Award, the Fire Fighter Award, and the Night Owl Award. At staff meetings, recipients are presented with certificates, a firefighter helmet, a stuffed owl, or a toy laser gun.

Hallway golf. Federated System Group occasionally indulges in an afternoon of "putt-putt" hallway golf. Employees pick their own foursome, bring a putter, and commence playing various holes down the hallways. Prizes are awarded for the best scoring individual and team.

Ideas online. BellSouth Mobility puts all its innovative ideas online. Volunteer "Quality Experts" work with the ideas if the persons submitting them cannot implement the ideas themselves.

Innovators Award. Create a monthly Innovators Award for people who come up with a usable innovative idea. Allow workers time for innovation and capture their creativity with a contest for the best idea of the month.

Humor corner. Give employees one corner of a break room or other area to post cartoons, illustrations, and other items designed to relieve stress. At the end of each week, the staff can award a prize for the best submission.

Best Practices | for Creating a Charged Work Environment

Crazy hat day. Create a special contest and have everyone wear the craziest hats to work.

Man Overboard Award. CIGNA believes in rewarding employees who go over and beyond for their customers. The Man Overboard Award is a life-saving ring that the president presents to an employee at a special ceremony. Teams whose implemented ideas improve productivity may receive awards as high as $25,000.

Employee dollars. Employees at Phoenix Solutions Inc. award an "employee dollar" to fellow employees who do something special or exceed company expectations. Each month the employee with the most dollars gets movie tickets, dinner, and a personalized "Employee of the Month" plaque.

Terrific Tuesday. When planning meetings or special projects, keep in mind that Monday is the least productive day of the week. Tuesday is the most productive day before the midweek slump begins on Wednesday and continues the rest of the week.

Generate competition. In the U.S. Air Force, the wing commander recognizes the airman, NCO, and Sr. NCO of the quarter at a quarterly Commander's Call. Nominations come from within each unit, which then works to support its nominee, thereby generating competition between units.

Birthday club. Energize employees with a Monthly Birthday Club celebration. At breaktime, serve special refreshments and recognize birthday celebrants with a card.

Lunch break. Have meals brought in occasionally. On the last Friday of the month, declare a longer lunch break and have pizza and beverages delivered to all.

Best Practices | for Creating a Charged Work Environment

Improve quality, cost, and performance. At Melroe Company, employees who submit ideas to improve quality, cost, and performance are eligible for a $90 gift certificate to Wal-Mart. At a yearly banquet for all contributors, the company also gives larger cash awards and items such as televisions.

Prescription | for Action

- Capture the creativity of people and have random drawings for the best idea of the month.
- Allow the person who came up with a winning idea to help form a team to implement it.
- Set the example and periodically do something unexpected.
- Surprise your workforce with a celebration of some kind.
- Build relationships and friendly competition between departments.
- Set challenging, but achievable goals.
- Appoint a "Director of Fun."
- Allow employees to visit similar organizations to capture new ways of accomplishing their work.
- Managers' performance evaluations should include a "new ideas implemented" section.
- Managers should be told and expected to listen to and implement ideas of their employees.
- Measure what is important and publicly display those measurements.
- Rotate people and have them work in other sections and departments at least one day a quarter.
- Reward and recognize people for breaking the rules (i.e., bureaucratic rules and procedures).

Chapter Eight

Performance Management Transforms Workers to Winners

I n my position, I hear lots of complaints. People tell me that the work ethic is declining . . . that people get hired and don't show up or skip shifts when they please . . . that it's getting harder to find competent and motivated workers with good attitudes. In effect, these gripers are saying, "These people are flawed, and there's nothing I can do about it."

The gripers are wrong. As I've stressed throughout this book, leaders can do plenty to turn an average—or even a poor—performer into a highly productive one. In a high-retention environment, leaders provide something called "discretionary effort." Basically, discretionary effort is what leaders *do* to create superior performance. It is situational and varies depending on the individual and circumstance. Reward and recognition and performance management are key elements of discretionary effort. Its influence can be substantial, as Figure 8.1 shows. Anyone with the knowledge, authority, and inclination—executives, managers, supervisors, even employees on the line—can create programs that improve the work environment and raise the performance bar.

Although the high-retentionship work environment offers many opportunities for transformation, this chapter and

Figure 8.1   Superior Performance

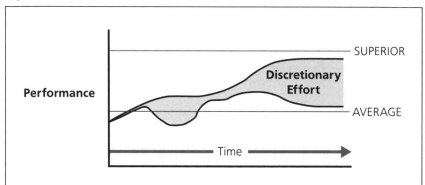

Chapter 9 look at two key elements that can profoundly affect productivity: (1) performance management and (2) recognition and reward.

Performance management is about creating an environment where people know what is expected of them, have access to the tools they need for their work, and are supported in their quest to do their best. It's about creating people who feel good about themselves and their accomplishments and in turn will reward the organization with loyalty and high retention.

Performance management has three key goals:

1. Creating a workplace where top performers want to stay
2. Transforming people who are not "stars" into top performers
3. Aligning behavior and actions toward the goals of the business enterprise

Each of these goals is important. Retention is especially important if you are in an industry that can't afford to pay top dollar for a top-notch workforce. Transforming nonperformers into stars becomes more critical as the workforce shrinks. And aligning behavior and actions with your business's goals is the bottom line for staying in business. You need to define and then create the behaviors that will ensure that the company runs at maximum efficiency and productivity.

To effectively manage performance, you need to determine what *performance* means and how to structure an environment to elicit it. When this spadework is finished, it's easy to design a recognition and reward program that reinforces performance at the back end.

But be careful. Performance management is not manipulation. People never respond well to control or manipulation and will flee an environment in which these strategies are dressed up as performance management.

However, performance management does seek to change behavior. After all, if you want to lose weight, you have to exercise and change eating habits. If you want to close a sale, you must first talk to a client. And if you want to nurture star performers, you need to identify and target the behaviors needed to bring success to your business.

A well-structured performance management program can do the following:

- Help people reach their potential.
- Encourage people to take risks to accept change.
- Build confidence.
- Align behavior with company goals, principles, and values.
- Even the playing field.
- Stimulate action.
- Create new habits.

How Joe Learned His Job

Let's begin with a little story about how employees learn what behavior is acceptable and their expectations at work.

The day that Joe Employee joins your company, he starts trying to determine what behavior is or is not acceptable. For the first two weeks, he experiments to see what happens if he comes to work late. Oops! The consequences are immediate. He is punished with a counseling statement or verbal warning.

Embarrassed, Joe decides to be the best employee of the company, a star performer. Like a shooting star, his performance leaps way above that of his coworkers. But nothing happens. Thirty days later, Joe knows what is acceptable and unacceptable in your company. He has figured out what behavior is rewarded and recognized and has started to settle in.

Unfortunately, he has learned that he'll get the same recognition, prestige, and reinforcement whether he is a top performer or just an average one. So he decides that it is safer and easier just to be average—a sad and harmful lesson to learn and reason enough to look for a job at a company that will recognize and reward his efforts.

To avoid this situation, implement the ABC model: antecedents, behavior, consequences.

The ABC Model: Antecedents, Behavior, Consequences

Early in my military career I went through airborne training, which teaches soldiers the proper and safe way to parachute from an airplane. At the end of the intensive three-week training program, students must make five successful parachute jumps. "Successful" in this case means being able to walk away after landing on the ground versus being carried off on a litter. The program succeeds in transforming motivated but unskilled and frightened solders into soldiers who are proud, physically fit, and able to repeat this behavior whenever the country requires it.

The word *behavior* is an important part of the ABC model, which I learned of from David Cheatham, a human resources manager at Coca-Cola. An effective way to understand how certain actions and conditions influence human behavior, the ABC model examines antecedents, behavior, and consequences. (See Figure 8.2.)

An antecedent creates actions or enables and motivates a person to *do* something. Behavior is what happens as a result of the antecedent: showing up for work on time, having per-

Figure 8.2   ABC Model

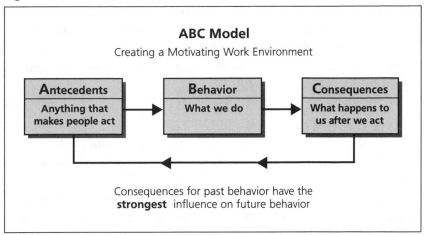

fect attendance, or properly completing a system network for a major corporation. Consequences are what happens to people after they act. They can be positive or negative and provide the incentive for repeating the behavior. Examples are reward or recognition, a feeling of satisfaction, confidence, or a new ability.

Let's say in Joe's case that he started coming to work late. A direct consequence of his behavior is needed; for Joe it should be a warning from his supervisor. If he comes to work late again, a written counseling statement is the consequence.

The ability to create and manage behaviors is critical if you want a high-retention workplace of top performers. To align behaviors with the goals of an organization, you need to create antecedents that elicit those behaviors and consequences that reinforce them.

In business, antecedents take the form of training programs, policies and procedures, mission and vision statements, guiding principles, rules and regulations, or organizational structure and hierarchy. A procedure manual may state that all vehicles will be painted white; a training program may stress good telephone manners or point out that a person who is late for work will receive a counseling statement. In the fast-food industry, strict guidelines and checklists ensure that almost anyone can follow and perform at a satisfactory level. These clear expectations shape the behavior of employees.

In airborne training, the antecedent that builds individual competence until the soldier feels confident to voluntarily jump (behavior) from the airplane is training. However, in some cases the soldier will not voluntarily exit the aircraft and a new antecedent (pushing or perhaps a large boot on the soldier's backside!) is needed to create the desired behavior (falling from the airplane).

For intrinsically motivated and competent individuals, consequences of behavior may be unimportant. But for individuals who are extrinsically motivated or are learning a new skill, consequences may determine whether a behavior increases or decreases. Furthermore, consequences can reliably ensure whether a behavior will occur again in the future.

In the final analysis, consequences are important when

- aligning behavior to organizational goals;
- making people feel appreciated;
- creating an environment where people can excel;
- creating and rewarding good work ethics;
- creating a feeling of pride and purpose; and
- reinforcing the learning process.

Several consequences reinforce behavior in airborne training. First, safety. People who fall from the air and don't get hurt will be able to return and jump once more. Each time they land safely, their confidence level increases. In fact, statistics show it is safer to parachute from an airplane than to drive your automobile in Atlanta, Georgia. A second consequence is a feeling of pride, purpose, and elitism. Only a small percentage of military personnel successfully complete the training and become airborne paratroopers. Their achievement is confirmed by the final consequence or reward: a small, metal emblem called paratrooper wings that, when worn on a uniform, indicate the soldier's membership in an elite group. I too earned my paratrooper wings.

Focus on the Right Thing: Antecedents

Pine Oaks Golf Course reinforces the behavior of cleanliness by giving employees one bag of range balls for every cup of cigarette butts they pick up and turn in. Grayson College Golf Course reinforces the behavior of attendance by giving employees a day off for every three weeks of perfect attendance. The day may be used whenever bad weather slows business on the course.

Many service industries use bonuses to reinforce the behavior of selling service agreements. A plumbing company, for example, might give technicians a flyer to hand out to clients. The flyer explains the service agreement and includes an incentive for using the coupon. Each flyer is coded to identify the technician. When the client calls, the call taker asks for the code and the technician receives a bonus.

While behavior-driven consequences like these work well, too much attention to consequences can be dangerous. Outcome management—that is, focusing more on managing consequences than on managing antecedents—tends to highlight negative consequences, such as blaming and inspections. When calling businesses, you frequently hear such recorded messages as, "We may record this conversation in order to ensure we are providing the best service possible." This message is a clear indicator of consequence-based management. Service centers find it more expedient to monitor past performance—after the fact—than to select and train people before the fact.

When your only strategy is to manage by consequences, your outcome may be an environment of fear. Employee manuals emphasize negative consequences. If you are late three times, X will happen. If you misuse company property, X will happen to you. Get the picture? If not, see Figure 8.3.

Figure 8.3 Beatings

The Wrong Way to Motivate People

The beatings won't stop until the morale improves!

OR ELSE!

High-retention companies focus on antecedents—a wiser and less costly approach. The late Dr. W. Edwards Deming, who launched the quality revolution in America, believed that designing quality into the process was less expensive than inspecting for quality afterward. He urged companies to manage antecedents by properly preparing people for their jobs through training processes, better selection procedures, properly working equipment, and orientation programs. "Do it right the first time" became a mantra for American businesses, which learned they could save millions of dollars by changing their manufacturing processes to fix problems up front instead of fixing rejects or replacing faulty products later.

As the airborne program shows, it's always smarter and cheaper to focus on antecedents instead of on consequences. The army's thorough training program means it doesn't have to take injured and demoralized soldiers off the drop zone to the hospital for extensive and expensive therapy!

Below is a letter e-mailed to me from an owner of a plumbing service business:

An Outside Opinion about Attitudes,
Hiring, and Behavior

I believe the successful businesses of the future will have a good handle on how to direct the behavior of attitudinal basket cases. We won't have the luxury of hiring new people with the attitudes and people skills we prefer.

That's why I think we need to be learning how to elicit proper behavior from whatever personnel we have. Behavior, not attitude, is what puts beans in the pot. Consider this personal example.

I believe I have a great attitude. I care about people and I love to bring them together with the things they want or need. That's how I make my living and according to the numbers, I'm good at it. However, it's not just my attitude that sells. I'm sure I could just walk out the door in my Bermuda shorts, unshaven, wearing a T-shirt and I'd be able to sell something to somebody. It would be slim pickings, though. I certainly wouldn't sell much that way.

I use behaviors to "grease things up" a bit. Being polite, using floor protectors and rugs, wearing neat uniforms, properly writing work orders, using price books ad infinitum are all behaviors that can be taught, monitored and inspected. Granted, many of these behaviors are simply common courtesy but apparently common courtesy is in short supply these days.

You might be able to recognize my good attitude because it's almost always there but you wouldn't be able to quantify it or make adjustments to it. That's up to me. You can, however, document every little behavior you expect me to perform. Further, you can demonstrate that my performance rides on how well I execute the behavior you expect. Whether I'm late for work because of a bad attitude or a flat tire, the numbers will show that a late start usually means missed opportunities. In other words, it's not the attitude; it's the action (behavior) that determines success or failure.

In our industry, we have the same hiring pool. By providing trouble-shooting checklists and procedures (behaviors), we can narrow down most technical problems to find a reasonable solution. Sure, there's a desperate need for technical expertise as well and those who have it will excel. But the majority of our revenue can be generated by "average" people who follow the rules.

By implementing service call procedures (behaviors), we can ensure that our valuable customer gets the treatment they deserve. Again, great attitudes will rise to the top but the majority of our revenue will come from average people who simply follow our rules. How well we develop and manage these rules will determine how successful our businesses will be.

Translating the ABC Approach into Performance Management: Bates Ace Hardware

Customers who walk through the doors of Bates Ace Hardware can easily sense the company's positive attitude. When a customer asks for an item, employees don't point—they escort people to the proper location. When more than three people are in line, an employee opens another cash register. Employees feel a sense of pride and teamwork. Both owners and employees worked together to create a totally new management philosophy that is reflected in every aspect of Bates's business.

Located on one of the busiest streets in downtown Atlanta, Bates has 32 employees, more than 20,000 square feet, and $3 million in sales. Owned by David Doss since 1973 and managed by David's son, Wade, this family-owned business serves a demanding market of homeowners and industrial customers.

Often, family-owned businesses do a poor job preparing the second generation for succession. After a store manager resigned, I was asked to help David and his son and daughter prepare a plan for the succession process. Initially, we came up with three major goals for the succession process:

1. A complete transition of store management
2. Raising the level of customer service
3. Creating a work environment where employees share ownership in the decision-making process

In most businesses, owners or managers make up and dictate the rules and then spend valuable time making others comply. Employees resist and quit, forcing management to keep finding and replacing employees—an expensive process. Because Amy and Wade wanted to have employees share ownership in the decision-making process, they invited employees to participate in the design process. A succession transition team of eight supervisors, office staff, and front-line employees worked with David, Amy, and Wade to chart the course for a new way of running the business. We reasoned that if employees could design something they liked, they would be more likely to support it and make it work. We were right. Ultimately, the transition team members became the strongest advocates with the highest job satisfaction.

After several off-site meetings, a plan began taking shape. One exercise used to guide the transition team was visualization. Team members were asked to close their eyes and imagine themselves as customers who walked into the "best hardware store in the world." Then they visualized how they want to be treated by the employees . . . what the employees were wearing . . . and what the store looked like. As each member spoke, we wrote his or her ideas down on a flip chart.

Next, team members were asked to visualize how it felt to be an employee of the "world's best company." Their visualizations were guided by questions like, "How do you want your co-workers to treat you?" "What type of supervisors do you want to work for?" "How are you shown appreciation?" All answers and ideas were screened, discussed, and summarized, and eventually became part of an overall strategic plan. The strategic plan became the road map for the transformation process.

Creating the Behavior of Good Customer Service

Because stores like Bates Ace Hardware need to deliver good service, customer service became one of the essential components of the strategic plan. The transition started by identifying the specific actions, attitudes, and behaviors employees need to take in order to deliver good service. Following a similar model used by the Ritz-Carlton hotels, the transition team designed the "20 Customer Service Commandments." Each commandment identified a trait or behavior the store wanted displayed when employees dealt with one another. To transform this exercise into reality, the team undertook the following guidelines:

Repetition.   The goal was to make the commandments a habit, part of the Bates Ace Hardware culture. To do this, the team printed the commandments on a small card for employees to keep with them while at work. Each day, a new commandment is selected and supervisors conduct a minitraining session on what the commandment means to them. Intermittently, supervisors quiz employees on the commandments.

Department inspections.   Making people accountable is the key to long-term success. At Bates, each employee had responsibility for one store department but little accountability. Shelves were sometimes empty and employees sometimes failed to resolve customer questions. To maintain accountability and ownership, the general manager and store managers instituted a monthly department inspection. The goal was to create some friendly competition between departments as well as keep the appearance and stock at proper levels. The winners of the inspection win $50 each month.

Creating new leaders.   The transition process created new leadership at all levels. During the meetings, we noticed the special talents, interests, and abilities of all the team members themselves. Two employees in particular—the cashier supervisor and a salesperson—exhibited great leadership potential. The team expanded their jobs and assumed new responsibilities as assistant store managers.

This move had a positive impact in several ways. First, it reduced costs by eliminating the need to hire an outside store manager. Furthermore, by training the new assistant store managers, the owners gained freedom from spending all their time on the floor. Finally, it improved the attitudes and the job satisfaction of both assistant store managers.

Putting the right people in the right jobs.   The old saying "One rotten apple spoils the whole barrel" is truer than ever before. When facing a hiring shortage, many businesses hire anyone walking through the front door. Bad mistake! One bad employee will spoil the attitudes of everyone on the team, turn away customers, and even steal you blind.

For Bates Hardware, hiring the right people was critical. Its owners knew from experience that one-on-one job interviews didn't reveal enough information for a manager to make a good selection. They wanted to go beyond the basic interview to find out more about the values and attitudes of the applicant.

With my firm's help, Bates joined the growing number of American companies now using personality and screening assessments on all job applicants. Bates implemented computerized applicant selection assessments that estimate a candidate's reliability, work ethic, and ability to provide a positive interface with customers. The system also evaluates the likelihood of the person sticking around longer than three months. Once the store started using assessments, the quality, attitude, and longevity of its employees improved dramatically.

Bates Ace Hardware
Customer Service Commandments

1. The vision statement will be known, owned, and energized by all employees.
2. Our motto is: "We go beyond the call of duty." Help coworkers and practice cross training to promote a positive work environment.
3. All employees shall practice the three steps of service.
   a. Demonstrate a friendly and caring attitude.
   b. Anticipate and exceed customer needs and expectations.
   c. Offer your business card and express your desire to help them in the future.
4. All employees will successfully complete Ace training and the National Hardware Course to ensure they understand how to perform to the Bates Hardware standards in their position.
5. Each employee will understand their work area and company goals.
6. All employees will know the needs of their customers and fellow employees so that we may offer the products and services they expect. Offer your business cards for any future needs.
7. Each employee shall regularly report defects throughout the store.
8. Any employee who receives a customer complaint "owns" the complaint.
9. Instant customer pacification will be ensured by all. React quickly to correct the problem immediately. Do everything you possibly can to never lose a customer.
10. The highest levels of cleanliness are the responsibility of every employee.
11. Treat every customer with respect and smile. We are on stage. Always make positive eye contact and use language like, "Good morning," "Certainly," "I'll be happy to," and "My pleasure."
12. Always speak well of your store in and out of the workplace.
13. Accompany a customer to the correct aisle instead of pointing to another area of the store.
14. Always use correct telephone etiquette. Answer the phone within three rings with a "smile" and avoid transfers when possible. If

necessary, ask the customer, "May I place you on hold?" Be knowledgeable of store merchandise and equipment.

15. Uniforms are to be immaculate: Wear proper and safe footwear (clean and polished) and your correct nametag. Take pride in your personal appearance.

16. Notify your supervisor of any hazards, injuries, equipment, or assistance that you need. Practice energy conservation and proper maintenance and repair of company property and equipment at all times.

17. It is every employee's responsibility to protect the assets of Bates Ace Hardware.

18. All employees are empowered to reward others for going beyond the call of duty.

19. All employees will be on time when reporting for their shift or returning from lunch or break.

20. Thou shalt carry the 20 commandments on thy person at all times when working.

Managing Performance through Employee Ownership: McKay Nursery

In my view, the best performance comes from workplaces where the employees share in the ownership, responsibility, management, and therefore success of the business. When employees personally feel pain or gain, the outcome is usually superior.

In high-retention organizations, employees feel strongly that their contributions have a direct impact on the performance of the organization, and they know they will somehow share in its rewards. McKay Nursery, located in Waterloo, Wisconsin, is a good example.

Like many nurseries and greenhouses, McKay Nursery has a tough time attracting and keeping its workforce. Work is hard, and turnover in the industry matches the food industry's. To solve its problem, McKay decided to do something different, and in 1984 it became an ESOP—an employee-owned company.

McKay has 60 full-time workers and 100 migrant workers during the growing season. The company has always been generous with benefits and was one of the first companies in the United States to provide overtime pay to migrant workers.

Pay is generous and migrant workers are eligible for stock options after they work 1,000 hours at the nursery. They are guaranteed at least 10 percent of their gross wages, but contributions have reached 25 percent during very good years. Contributions are made in company stock or in cash that workers can invest in various mutual funds. After five years on the job, workers may make withdrawals but only for college tuition, bills, home purchases, or retirement.

As a result of this plan and the innovative leadership at McKay Nursery, 90 percent of the migrant workers return each year. Some have been with McKay for as long as 20 years. The plan effectively attracts new workers and motivates them to achieve productivity levels that exceed standards in the nursery business.

Financial Incentives for Performance and Retention

Financial incentives are a way to reward, reinforce, and recognize successful performance. Many kinds of incentive plans are available; some work, some don't.

I believe employees should share in the financial success as well as the hardship of an organization. Many organizations offer no incentive to work any harder than necessary—"You get the same paycheck no matter what you do in this job." A financial incentive plan may boost productivity, allow you to get extra effort, and gain a little more "ownership" from your employees.

If you have employees who only want to work for you because of the paycheck, then you are already in a tough situation. A performance bonus plan may keep these employees from leaving. If that's what it takes, so be it.

Performance Bonus Plans

A bonus system must be carefully designed to create the necessary consequences. Performance bonus plans are designed to create a feeling of ownership among the employees in the company. Complicated or simple, their goal is to create an environment in which employees can see how their contribution (i.e., their work) directly affects their paycheck each month.

The bonus plan can be designed to make payouts to employees on a periodic basis based on the profitability of the company. Special additions and deductions can be made based on individual and company performance, as the sample plan in the box below indicates.

Here are the key elements of creating a successful bonus plan:

- Incentives are paid in a timely manner.
- Employees feel a direct connection to their actions and the bonus they receive.
- Performance measurements are open to all and validated by the team.
- Performance measurements are fair.
- The program is communicated well and understood by all.
- The financial reward is proportionate to the level of performance.

Outline of Performance Bonus Plan

General Guidelines
- Base the bonus pool on monthly profits.
- Establish a threshold to be reached (5 to 10 percent) before the plan goes into effect.
- Establish a percentage of profit to be paid to employees.
- Deductions are made on the threshold.
- Each employee's bonus will have individual deductions made.
- The total bonus will be divided equally among the employees.

- Decide who is eligible (e.g., must be employed for one month, etc.).

Individual Deductions
- One unexcused absence: 25 percent deduction
- Failure to attend company meeting: 10 percent deduction
- Two or more unexcused absences: 100 percent deduction
- Counseling statement: 25 percent deduction

Company Deductions
- Rejects greater than 0.10: 10 percent deduction
- Customer complaints greater than 0.20: 20 percent deduction

Individual Additions
- Customer writes letter of appreciation: 5 percent addition
- Employee quits smoking: 5 percent addition
- Employee attends education course: 10 percent addition
- Awarded by peer: 5 percent addition

Using Bonuses to Retain IT Personnel: Atlas Editions

Many IT companies use retention bonuses to prevent people from leaving at critical times. Atlas Editions, a technology company, used a successful bonus plan during a major 18-month-long project. It needed the team to complete the project and couldn't afford for anyone to quit. Atlas created benchmarks, established dates when each phase of the project was to be completed, and tied financial payouts to the project phases. Ten percent of the total bonus was paid out after six months; 20 percent was paid after one year so long as the milestones were completed on schedule; and 70 percent was paid after 18 months, when the project was complete, debugged, tested, and operational. The top three managers were liable for a 10 percent deduction penalty for each month the project was delayed.

Each team member received anywhere from 15 to 55 percent of his or her base pay depending on technical level, management experience, and involvement in the project. As a result, no one departed and the project was completed on time.

How Nucor Steel Rewards Performance and Productivity

Nucor Steel, with 7,000 nonunion employees and nearly $4.5 billion in sales, is one of the few remaining steel companies in the United States. To remain competitive in its industry, it focuses on two clear goals: (1) building steel manufacturing facilities economically and (2) operating the facilities productively.

To achieve these goals, Nucor has streamlined and decentralized management and allows each plant to operate as an independent business unit. Only four layers of management exist to cover hourly employees: chairman, vice chairman and president; vice president-general manager; department managers; and supervisors/professionals. Only 22 employees—8 managers and 14 administrative employees—work in the corporate headquarters. Senior executives do not have company cars, dining rooms, executive parking spaces, or corporate jets. Everyone from the janitors to the CEO has the same basic but generous benefits plan.

Nucor's employee relations philosophy is simple and effective:

- Employees should have the opportunity to earn according to their productivity.

- If employees do their job well today, they should have a job tomorrow. (Nucor hasn't laid off employees in 28 years.)

- Employees have a right to be treated fairly. The company listens to employees through crew meetings, department meetings, shop dinners, and employee surveys.

- Employees must have an avenue of appeal if they believe they have been treated unfairly. This complaint procedure allows employees to carry their complaints to the president of the company.

Nucor backs up its philosophy with a unique pay-for-performance compensation system. Salaried employees receive 0 to 25 percent of their salary based on the return on assets (ROA) of their plant. Employees earn money based on their individual productivity. Although employees are paid an average hourly rate that is lower than the industry rate, they qualify for an exceptional performance bonus if they exceed hourly quotas. For example, the steel industry average considers that an individual should be able to straighten ten tons of steel an hour. Nucor's goal is to straighten eight tons an hour; and employees get an additional 5 percent bonus for every ton over eight they can straighten. They typically average 35 to 40 tons an hour. However, if they come to work late, they lose their bonus for the day. And if they miss a day of work during the week, they lose their bonus for the entire week.

Department managers also have base salaries that are lower than those of other plants. But they qualify for an annual bonus based on their plant's ROA, which varies from 0 to 82 percent of their salary. They get an additional bonus based on the weekly production of their crew of 100 to 200 percent of base salary.

Senior officers have one compensation system. They do not participate in profit sharing, pensions, bonuses, or retirement plans, and their base salaries are also set below the industry average. They receive one annual bonus based on the return of shareholders' equity above certain minimum earnings. Composed of 60 percent in stock and 40 percent in cash, the bonus ranges from zero to several hundred percent of salary.

This unique way of rewarding productivity keeps Nucor's productivity high and its absenteeism low. Employees see a direct correlation between what they do and their paychecks— a major incentive and a key strength of the program. In fact, the program prompts such high performance that employees were refusing to take time off. The company began forcing them to take the time by giving them four extra days off a year. Even so, only half the employees use their four extra days!

Best Practices | for Performance Management

Lottery system. One company used a lottery system to reduce absenteeism by 75 percent and costs by 62 percent. Only employees with no absenteeism during the month can participate; prizes include a television, a bicycle, and so on.

Play poker. Another company used poker to improve attendance. Each day that employees come to work, they can draw one playing card. Those who attend all week own five cards on Friday. The player with the best hand wins $20.

Perfect attendance program. One large rental business encourages attendance by giving an employee with perfect attendance during the year $300, a limo ride to a restaurant for a free dinner with his or her spouse, and a gift certificate worth $100.

Managing absent or late employees. Set up a Potential Earned Bonus Account for each employee for a set amount, say $500. Every day an employee is late but calls in to tell you, $10 is deducted from the account. Every day he or she is late and does not call in, $15 is deducted. Every day an employee is absent but calls in gets a penalty of $25. And every time an employee is absent and doesn't call in, $35 is taken away. I know of one company that installed a huge red light outside the office and turned it on at 8:00 AM to let employees know they are late as they drive in.

Standing ovations. At S. C. Johnson Wax, employees nominate fellow workers in their department for a special award. Each week the entire department stops work, goes to the awardee's cubicle or work area, and gives him or her a standing ovation. The person who nominated the winner presents the winner with a Good Work certificate and tells what he or she did to win the award.

Best Practices | for Performance Management

Attendance awards. Employees of Gwinnett County (Georgia) receive perfect attendance certificates for not missing a day of work during the month. This successful program made a significant improvement in the absenteeism level among employees. It was so successful, in fact, that some employees weren't keeping doctor appointments because it would make them ineligible for the monthly award. The county recognized the unavoidable need to occasionally have appointments during the business day and instituted a second award for people who miss less than eight hours a month. This allowed employees to go to the doctor but still retain an incentive to take a few hours off rather than the entire day.

Champion the champion. This item is on the agenda at every meeting of J. C. Penney Insurance Group at all levels up to the president. At every meeting, someone is singled out and recognized for a special accomplishment. The presentation explains what the person did and how that activity had an impact on others.

Service over and above requirements (SOAR). At Nationwide Insurance, customers, managers, and peers nominate employees for service "over and above." Regional six-member boards (all volunteers) meet weekly or monthly to review the nominations and select a winner. The winner chooses a prize from a catalog that includes magnets, pins, mugs, writing pens, and sweatshirts.

Best Practices | for Performance Management

Reusable-coffee-mug program. In an effort to educate the community about environmental issues, officials from Clifton, New Jersey, made a reusable coffee mug. They figured that most people throw away 624 coffee cups a year, creating a massive burden on the environment. Their efforts focused on reducing the amount of disposable coffee cups and other forms of litter. The city gave these reusable mugs to merchants and "mom and pops" who sold coffee. The merchants agreed to sell the coffee at a discount to customers who returned with their mugs.

Greased Monkey Award. At First American, managers present a Greased Monkey Award to the computer technician who is best in resolving problems with computer programs. The award is a plastic toy monkey in a jar of Vaseline along with a $50 dinner certificate.

Prescription | for Action

- Be clear on what expectations people are to reach.
- Clarify how a supervisor's performance will be measured.
- Have company executives share their expectations with your managers.
- Hold managers accountable and responsible for retention.
- Tie rewards and recognition to performance results.
- Avoid arbitrary and unfair measurement systems.
- Ensure individuals have the tools and training to make improvements.
- Eliminate the element of fear in performance management.
- Tear down walls and barriers between departments.
- Maintain a list of organizational improvement priorities and action plans.

Chapter Nine

Reward and Recognition Programs Lead to Higher Retention

Recognition: A form of sincere praise or appreciation given to an individual by another.

Reward/Award: An earned item of value presented to an individual for successful accomplishment of a particular service, task, or mission.

Maria had worked in the quality assurance department for months. In addition to doing her job well, she voluntarily came in early each day and had coffee ready for the rest of the team. Making coffee wasn't in her job description, but it was something she wanted to do and it made her feel good. She enjoyed her job and planned to stay as long as possible. Maria's supervisor, Joan, was the type of person who noticed things and always had a positive word to say. Joan would even brag about her employees in front of her district manager, Mr. Cramer.

At dinner, Maria would tell her family that Joan was the reason she liked working there. Joan made her feel good about what she did. She noticed and recognized the little things people did and always had something nice to say to them. Maria knew she could find a better-paying job closer to her home, but she planned to stay as long as Joan was her boss.

Salonda had the opposite experience. An administrative assistant who had worked for a large organization for 22 years, she had shouldered more and more responsibility as her company downsized time and again. She felt as if she had five times as much work.

The last straw was when the company cut a temporary worker who worked with her. Salonda told her boss she didn't see how she could get all the work done. Instead of acknowledging her workload or seeking a solution, he casually remarked, "You will figure out a way." The next day Salonda quit. Now she's a floor clerk at a local homebuilding store. She makes half the money—but has twice the fun and feels her efforts are recognized rather than ignored.

The moral of these stories? Money may attract people to the front door, but something else keeps them from going out the back. Although many people claim they are quitting for a better-paying job elsewhere, survey after survey shows that a lack of appreciation and recognition is a primary reason why people quit their jobs. Another survey by Robert Half lists "limited recognition and praise" as the number one reason employees leave. "Compensation" is second.

Reward and recognition are not just nice things to do. They're key elements in the retention model. People have a basic need to feel valued and appreciated. Properly designed reward and recognition programs help to meet that need.

What are the reasons you stay at your present job?
    Feel appreciated for what I do   35%
    Makes me feel good   27%
What causes you the greatest dissatisfaction at work?
    Lack of appreciation   33% (the leading answer!)

Source: Chart Your Course Workforce Retention Survey.

Why Reward and Recognition Work

There are many reasons why a reward and recognition program is such an effective strategy for retaining employees. For starters, reward and recognition programs are simple to administer. They don't cost much, don't take much time, and don't complicate the payroll; moreover, they are flexible. Informal recognition programs can recognize outstanding behavior quickly; more formal programs can reinforce behavior over the long run. Finally, they can accelerate the learning process, especially for new or younger workers, who often need plenty of reinforcement.

These programs are especially important in situations in which effort cannot be rewarded with money or promotions. Governmental organizations and nonprofits, for example, often find their ability to give promotions or raises is restricted. Once, when I spoke to the civilian workforce of the U.S. Marine Corps, I discovered that whereas active duty members were acknowledged with ribbons and other formal recognition, the civilian workforce felt underappreciated.

A well-administered program also builds camaraderie and values and makes people feel good about themselves and their job. But the biggest reason for the success of these programs is simple: they allow people to celebrate success and feel good about who they are and whom they work for. As people spend more and more time at work, celebrating success and making people feel good are more and more critical. People want to be appreciated as individuals as well as appreciated for their jobs. Rarely do people feel overappreciated for what they do.

Yet many managers do a poor job of complimenting others—much less celebrating success! That's because reward and recognition make some managers nervous, even fearful. They may fear offending someone or leaving someone out. If no one else is doing it, they may not want to be the first to take the plunge. Simple praise may make them uncomfortable.

In situations like these, a nudge from the top can be very effective. I know a hospital CEO who gives his managers five tokens at the beginning of each weekly staff meeting. Their instructions are to go out in the hospital and give the tokens to people they catch doing something good. They may not come back to the following week's staff meeting until they give away all of their coins.

Often, managers get so involved with day-to-day business that they forgo the soft skills that are so important to people. The tokens served as a reinforcement to start this behavior.

Elements of an Effective Program

An effective recognition and reward program recognizes and appreciates the efforts of individuals while taking into account their individual needs, differences, and personalities.

In our complex, diverse workforce, managers need to understand and recognize individual needs as well as group needs. A one-size-fits-all approach to recognition simply won't work. In the army, individuals leaving one assignment for another traditionally received a plaque. After countless assignments, I had boxes and boxes of plaques. I was tired of them, and my wife didn't want them on the wall at home. Needless to say, plaques lost all of their appeal to me.

Before you plan your program, find out what motivates your people. Don't assume you already know. In one organization I worked with, management was absolutely certain that employees would select money as its preferred form of recognition. It turned out, money didn't matter but parking did. While executives and certain top employees could park in the lot next to the building, most employees had to park several blocks away. With this information in hand, we built a very effective program around parking.

Use the Individual Retention Profile discussed in Chapter 11 to grasp and understand the preferences of the people who work for or with you. The ultimate method of adapting the program to an individual is to let people select their own rewards. One employee may choose cash as a reward for achieving a goal; another employee may choose time off instead.

Another key aspect of an effective program is variety. All programs become a little boring after about six months. Add variety to your program to make it new and interesting. Consider friendly competitions between departments or unusual award items.

At Miami-based Creative Staffing, owner Ann Machado offers employees a menu of rewards, which includes parties, expensive dinners, chauffeured shopping sprees, spa sessions, and cooking lessons with Paul Prudhomme. Employees decide what they want, figure out how much their package costs, and determine how much additional business they have to generate to cover those costs. And they really enjoy choosing their own reward!

There are two forms of motivation: intrinsic and extrinsic. An effective program mixes intrinsic and extrinsic motivational tools. Intrinsic motivation, the highest form of motivation, comes from internal sources: the heart, soul, and mind. People who are intrinsically motivated do what they are supposed to do with little or no external pressure or influence. In my view, intrinsic motivation is a key element of the high-retention workplace. Every chapter in this book describes an ingredient in the mix that managers can use to create a working environment that allows everyone to be intrinsically motivated.

But in spite of a manager's best efforts, some people still need an extra prod to be productive. For these people, the "carrot and stick" approach of extrinsic motivation may be more appropriate, especially when someone is learning new skills or a new behavior.

In its most basic form, extrinsic motivation can appear to be a form of a bribe. Many incentives are bribes—"You do this and you get this." The best reward and recognition programs offer exciting and creative incentives in a high-productivity, high-retention context. If a company has hired people who already are intrinsically motivated and have good attitudes, their motivation and reward will be derived from doing a job in a positive work environment. Don't get carried away or grow overly dependent on gimmicks that have little value and importance to your people.

I know several companies that have relied so heavily on incentives that before any action is taken, employees ask,

"What's in this for me?" They have robbed their employees of the intrinsic motivation of pride and self-respect—a dangerous malady that is very difficult to change. Too many gimmicks and too much extrinsic motivation will eventually harm their creativity and initiative.

Reward and recognition must go beyond gimmicks. They must also go beyond insincere general comments like, "Keep up the good work." Of course, it's important to acknowledge the worth of employees at all levels. But shallow or routine praise given simply because "that's what the book says to do" is easy for employees to recognize and can do more harm than good.

Warning: Reward and Recognition Cannot Replace Leadership

As I've stressed throughout this book, leadership is the compass that keeps people focused and heading in the right direction. A leader's job is to remove barriers and obstacles that prevent people from doing their best.

If leadership is absent, no amount of money, incentives, or benefits will replace or make up for it. Too often, companies think that slapping a few colorful, inspirational posters on the wall is all it takes to motivate. They're wrong. Artwork like this is fine, but it can never be management's only approach to motivation. This is like rearranging deck chairs on the *Titanic.* The ship is foundering.

Basic Flavors of Reward and Recognition

Although there are literally thousands of variations on reward and recognition programs, all of them can be sorted into two categories: formal and informal. Both formal and informal programs can use financial and nonfinancial awards.

Informal programs are the easiest and most manageable. They are less structured, are more spontaneous, and are more likely to use praise to recognize and reward people. Managers, employees, or team members may recognize one another through tokens of appreciation and other programs that emphasize recognition over cash rewards. The most popular forms of *informal recognition* are listed below:

- Verbal praise
- Time off
- Letters of appreciation
- Shirts, mugs, key chains, and other items imprinted with the company logo
- Certificates and plaques
- Ceremonial coins
- Comments from customers
- Pizza and ice cream parties
- Tickets to sports events
- Access to decision makers
- Picnics and outings
- Parking spaces
- Special meals as a group
- Surprise celebrations
- Handwritten notes
- Movie tickets
- Peer recognition

Formal reward and recognition programs are more structured and recur more often than do informal programs; and they may use merchandise, money, travel, and other perks to recognize accomplishments and performance. The most typical forms of formal recognition are listed below:

- Travel awards
- Paid vacations to special locations
- Annual award ceremonies
- Employee-of-the-month selection

- Awards based on performance
- Service-related awards based on longevity/seniority
- Sales incentives
- Achievement awards
- Financial awards

Peer Recognition: Employees Reward Each Other

One of the easiest and most effective programs to initiate, peer recognition gives employees the power to reward each other for doing a good job. It works because employees themselves know who works hard and deserves recognition. After all, managers can't be everywhere all the time, and employees are in the best position to catch people doing the right things. Also, as a result of peer pressure, workers usually value each other's influence more than that of their supervisor's.

In local government organizations, workers often face limited job opportunities and pay raises. Recognizing this, the Gwinnett County Tax Commissioner's office, in Lawrenceville, Georgia, developed a motivation program called "Shining Stars" that helped workers make each other feel good about their accomplishments.

Instead of pay raises and promotions, employees are given an unlimited supply of Shining Star forms to handwrite a little note about a coworker's good job. On the back of the form is a list of behaviors such as:

- Demonstrates friendly, caring service
- Shows flexibility
- Demonstrates teamwork
- Helps to save money

Completed forms are handed directly to the coworker or sent through interoffice mail. At the end of the month the department holds a ceremony for everyone recognized. The employee who received the highest number of forms gets an extra nod and a special gift from the commissioner.

All the month's forms are put into a basket and names are randomly drawn for additional prizes. The forms are read aloud and recognition given to both the awardee as well as the person who submitted the form. The winners also randomly draw their prizes out of another basket.

In its "Thank You Coupon" program, the Texas Credit Union gives each employee seven coupons a year to give to any employees they wish to recognize for going out of their way to help customers or fellow employees. The coupons are redeemed for $10 certificates for food, movies, golf, and the like. Everyone in the company, from the president and vice presidents down, is eligible for a coupon.

These informal peer recognition programs offer several advantages over other formal recognition programs. They work best when the *Fast-Fun* formula, shown in Figure 9.1, is followed:

Focus on the behavior you want to reward. A reward and recognition program must target specific behaviors that are important to the organization. Whether it is teamwork or customer service, define ahead of time the behavior you are looking for.

Avoid bureaucratic judging and committees. When committees and boards make decisions, someone feels cheated. Charges of unfairness will surface. In the Gwinnett County program and other peer recognition programs, the random drawing is a key element. Except for the person who gets the highest quantity of forms, every other "winner" is by the luck of the draw.

Simplicity. When it comes to peer recognition, the simpler the better. The easier the program is to run, the more likely it will work. After about six months, you may want to consider changing the program to maintain interest and enthusiasm.

Figure 9.1 Fast Fun

FAST FUN

F-Focus on Behavior

A-Avoid Judging

S-Simple

T-Team Owned

Fun!

*T*eam ownership. Peer recognition works best when employees run and own the program. Team ownership removes the onus from the supervisor and allows the team to manage it—where it belongs.

*F*UN. Make the peer recognition program as fun, entertaining, and spontaneous as possible.

Gwinnett County's program works because it meets all these criteria. It targets behaviors that employees believe are important. It avoids creating one winner and dozens of losers. It's simple, and the 30-minute award presentation is fun and leaves people feeling charged up and ready to go back to work.

Online Reward and Recognition Programs

Imagine sitting at your laptop and receiving an e-mail message saying you won the new idea contest. Attached to the message is a $49 voucher for a gift available anywhere on the Internet, redeemable immediately.

Online incentive programs like this are growing rapidly because they are fast, flexible, and in many cases cheaper than traditional reward and recognition programs. Unlike traditional programs, online programs let participants instantly track progress, check contest standings, and redeem rewards. They are especially effective in meeting the needs of those who have nontraditional work arrangements and work at home, telecommute, or are stationed away from the central office.

Online programs are great for a workforce that is technosavvy but won't work for those who are not. Consider the demographics of your workforce. If your workforce uses computers and Internet technology, an online program would work. If your people aren't comfortable with computers, stick to a traditional program. Keep the program simple. The fewer options or choices, the better. Of course, choices for the recipient should meet the needs of, or connect with, the individual.

You can streamline your own work by enlisting an online vendor to provide complete administration of the program. One vendor can provide everything from record-keeping and forms to tax administration and tracking. One possibility is CardEx.com, which provides a prepaid debit MasterCard that allows people to choose their own rewards wherever Master-Card is accepted (a virtual MasterCard debit card that can be purchased and delivered online and used wherever Master-Card can be accepted on the Internet) or a rechargeable Incen-tiveCard debit card that allows recipients to shop worldwide. CardEx can be contacted via telephone at 800-765-2991 or at their Web site, <www.CardEx.com>.

Flooz.com offers e-mail gift dollars or "Flooz" that can be redeemed for merchandise from over 60 online stores such as Godiva Chocolatier, Barnes & Noble, and Brookstone. Gifts are delivered via e-mail with a personal message and online greeting card. For more information, visit <www.flooz.com>. Please refer to Appendix C for a source list of organizations providing incentive items for reward and recognition.

Tips for Running a Successful Online Program

- Show employees it is easy to use. Encourage your employees to browse the Internet site to gain familiarity.
- Communicate the importance of reward and recognition to your employees. Make sure senior management uses the program and can talk about it in their meetings. Send weekly e-mails about the program to your employees.
- Be consistent in the use of the program. If you want to recognize employees' birthdays, make sure all departments use the online program to do this.

Formal Reward and Recognition Programs

Traditional Employee-of-the-Month Programs: Not Recommended

I have seen very few Employee-of-the-Month programs work as intended. The intended results fall short and, in some cases, the program can do more harm than good. Why?

Fairness is the main problem. Any program that selects only one winner is bound and determined to make others feel like losers. Also, employees must be nominated to be considered. But what happens to people whose manager doesn't want to take the time to nominate anyone? What happens to people who telecommute or work outside the traditional work environment? Honoring one person also defeats the concept of teamwork. To encourage and reward teamwork, consider selecting a Team of the Month.

One organization I worked with was a dental organization whose Employee-of-the-Month program was not working. Every month one person was nominated for selection. A committee of eight senior managers selected the winner and awarded him or her a savings bond. I found several weaknesses with the program. First, the winner did not really feel like a winner. Second, many people were not nominated and not only felt ignored but also felt they were just as deserving as or, in some cases, more deserving than the winner. Finally, the deciding committee would not let any one clinic have a winner twice in a row so they arbitrarily allowed a different clinic to win each month.

The organization followed our recommendation to allow the employees the opportunity to redesign a better system. We convened a problem-solving team of volunteers from each clinic. At our first meeting, we outlined options they could consider and then left them to decide.

An hour or two later they asked me to come back in. What they recommended was brilliant. The team proposed using a peer-rating system so that each month the team, not management, would select the best employee. They also recommended having six separate Employee-of-the-Month programs, one for each clinic. The team decided to collect money from the employees to buy a plaque for each clinic to display the names of each month's winners for all to see. Finally, the team would take the winner out for breakfast.

If management had suggested this idea, it might have flopped. But this new, employee-owned program was a success. The results were a fairer, more motivating program that empowered the workers and cost less money and time!

Achievement Awards

Achievement awards, on the other hand, are quite effective. An achievement award is something an individual earns through extra training, certification, or testing. The final outcome is a win–win for both the employee and the organization. The employee gains additional prestige for receiving this additional achievement, and the organization wins because it gains a more qualified, competent employee who is proud of a particular accomplishment.

In the military, soldiers always have the opportunity to achieve certain designations. I remember attempting to earn the Expert Field Medical Badge (EFMB), in a difficult week-long achievement test. People who successfully completed the test received a special badge to wear on their uniform. I have seen people literally push themselves to the point of exhaustion to win this badge. However, winning the award was less important than the process of learning the skills to complete the test: competence in all aspects of emergency medicine.

Merchandise Awards

Merchandise awards are given to individuals for accomplishing goals. Most programs award points or credits based on performance. The higher the performance, the greater the number of points. Points may be redeemed in some kind of gift catalog offering an array of awards based on the earned point value. Employees may redeem points online or by mailing the award certificate to the vendor, who usually handles all the administrative costs associated with the program and bills the company for all awards redeemed.

Yamaha, located in Newnan, Georgia, runs a merchandise program without an outside vendor. Like many Japanese companies, Yamaha practices traditional Japanese Kaizen. The plant, which manufactures golf carts and jet ski boats, has trained its workforce to identify and improve processes. The first step is for the employee to identify and photograph the broken process. The person then completes a Kaizen form, attaches the photograph, and forwards it to the Kaizen office for scoring. The Kaizen is awarded points based on the value of the idea.

Employees receive recognition including a special enamel pin and Yamabucks, which they redeem at the company store. To further reinforce the concept, they have random drawings at the end of the month for additional winners.

For more information on Kaizen, consider these sources:

Kaizen: The Key to Japan's Competitive Success, M. Imai, McGraw-Hill.

   Continuous Improvement: Quality Control Circles in Japanese Industry, P. Lillrank and N. Kano, Center for Japanese Studies, University of Michigan. Kaizen Institute Web site: <www.kaizen-institute.com/>.

Bobcat of Kentucky, a construction equipment company located in Louisville, Kentucky, takes employee recognition to new heights. It practices a combination of informal and formal awards that lead to high retention. Each year on the anniversary of their hire date, employees receive a cake and $100 for each year of service in a check made out to the Snap-On Tool Company. Bobcat rewards employee safety records with a Safety Bonus Program that screens each employee's driving record twice a year. Anyone who has a citation is removed from the program. At the end of the year the ones who remain get to split $2,000. Finally, employees' children who show an all-As report card receive a $50 savings bond. Who would want to quit this company!

How to Develop a Formal Reward and Recognition Program

Tallulah Falls, a breathtaking and scenic part of the Blue Ridge Mountains, drop approximately 1,200 feet into the Tallulah River. The gorge below is beautiful but dangerous; many people have ventured into it and never returned. Many years ago the tightrope walker The Great Wallenda decided to walk across the 1,000-foot-wide gorge. Unbelievably, he succeeded—steadying himself on the one-inch-thick cable with a 35-pound balancing pole. Asked to name the hardest part of this feat, he answered, "The first three steps."

   Starting a reward and recognition program is a lot less hazardous, but the hardest part of implementation is the first three steps. Once you're beyond them, the rest is easy.

Here are some steps to follow when setting up a formal program.

Step 1: Focus on the desired behavior or the goal of the program.   Begin with a clear, briefly stated goal, such as improved attendance, loyalty, or reduced accidents. Make sure the goal is specific, simple, quantifiable, measurable, and obtainable. Complicated goals can't be achieved. Neither can goals that are set too high above current performance. The goals need to be fair and reachable for the target group.

Step 2: Select an implementation team.   Appoint a committee of employees or ask for volunteers to obtain recommendations from the people who will be affected by the recognition effort. It is important to include people from all levels of the organization. Use an outside expert, if necessary, to facilitate the process. Let the team help set the goals, determine the performance factors, and report any obstacles to improvement.

Another effective strategy, depending on the size of the organization, is to appoint one coordinator for each branch or department. Coordinators provide direct support and information to their respective departments.

Step 3: Outline a strategy.   Build the foundation of the program carefully. Decide on the methodology to be used as well as the beginning date and the ending date. Focus on the target audience and anyone else who will be affected by the program. Decide whether the program will be employee or management driven. Employee-driven programs—like peer recognition programs—are the best and easiest to carry out. Allow adequate planning time, and create a specific implementation schedule. Ensure there is enough time to achieve the desired objectives or goals. Write the rules of the program carefully to avoid misunderstandings.

Step 4: Pick the type of recognition or award.   Provide adequate resources before you start the program. It is important that awards be perceived as being worth the effort required from the eligible participants. The power and influence of the award/recognition is minimized if the individual does not care about receiving it. Spend time discussing awards with the target group and select an award within the designated budget. Better yet, select several types of awards/recognition and allow the winners to choose.

Step 5: Develop a communication strategy.   The communication strategy is the most important and usually the most overlooked step in this process. Far more energy, time, and money usually go into the first four steps of this process than into the communication strategy. It's no surprise, then, that most programs fail because of poor communication. Inertia is difficult to change, but a solid communication plan will make all the steps work together, bringing life to the reward and recognition program.

The plan should address how, when, and how frequently people will be told about the program. An important time to discuss the plan is during the new employee orientation program.

Keep in mind that every program has a life cycle. The best programs have fixed beginning and ending dates. Also, the amount of energy placed on the program will have a great impact on the life cycle as well as on the success or failure of the program. Decide how to emphasize, and remind employees of, the program throughout its duration. Early in the process you should address:

- Why the program is needed
- How it will make a difference
- Eligibility requirements
- What participants have to do to win the award/recognition

During midcycle, highlight success stories of those who have participated. Post statistics and results of the program and send them to all employees via letters, company newsletters, e-mail, and announcements made during staff meetings.

Step 6: Kick off the program with gusto. The thrust of the kickoff is to focus attention on the goals of the program. Time the kickoff to get maximum participation. Stage an event where as many people as possible can come. Involvement and commitment from the senior executive is critical. It is important to have the senior executive speak to the employees about the program.

Step 7: Create a meaningful presentation strategy. The presentation strategy is critical to the program's overall success. It has two objectives: (1) to show appreciation to the awardee and (2) to encourage other employees to try for the award. In general, the presentation shows employees how important their effort is to the organization. A slipshod, poorly designed strategy tells people that their effort is not valued.

Step 8: Improve and change the program. The implementation team's job is not over until the program is evaluated. Collect data from awardees and coordinators on how the program can be improved. Determine whether the program achieved its stated objectives and goals. Have someone prepare a written evaluation of the program; and begin planning for the next program.

Precautions to Take When Considering Consequence-Based Programs

Not everyone believes that consequence-based programs are good. Some, like Alfie Kohn, the author of *Punished by Rewards,* believe that positive reinforcement, praise, reward, and recognition can be harmful to people.

Kohn opposes most forms of reward and recognition because his research shows that behavior-based programs don't work well with humans. His findings can be broken down into six statements:

1. Pay isn't a motivator.
2. Rewards punish.
3. Rewards rupture relationships.
4. Rewards ignore reasons.
5. Rewards reduce risk taking.
6. Rewards undermine intrinsic motivation.

Kohn's findings disturb many people, perhaps because incentives so permeate our society. Every organization, from the Boy Scouts to dot.com companies, engages in some kind of incentive-based system. And while I believe reward and recognition are effective, I also know there are limits to their effectiveness. Many reward programs guarantee only temporary compliance, not lasting change. Used incorrectly, rewards, recognition, praise, and bonuses can be manipulative and controlling and amount to little more than a bribe for behavior. In many instances, these behaviorist techniques create an effect opposite from that intended.

It's true that rewards can undermine intrinsic motivation. I've seen companies wipe out initiative and turn their employees into Pavlov's dog sitting ready for the next bone thrown their way.

The best form of recognition is still the ability to perform one's job to one's utmost ability, but the workforce is different today. When workers have shaky work ethics or lack qualified managers to lead them, focusing on consequences may be appropriate. But remember, goal setting and training should have a greater impact on productivity than rewards and recognition.

Best Practices | for Reward and Recognition

Plane tickets for employees. Buy all your materials with a credit card that gets airline miles. At the end of the year, trade in the miles for tickets for employee family members. They get to travel—and you don't have to pay! Employees are responsible for hotel and food. This practice is especially delightful to spouses who have longed for a vacation.

Shoot them a star. Before it closed, a division of J.C. Penney presented employees with a six-by-six-inch cardboard star that said, "YOU are a star performer." Details of what the person did to earn the recognition were printed on the back.

"I noticed" recognition. Have employees notice each other for exceptional jobs. At the end of each month, put names of "noticed" employees in a box. Hold a drawing and award a $50 gift certificate to the winner. Take a photograph of the winner and post it on a bulletin board for everyone to see during the next month.

"Kudograms." Give employees a supply of thank-you notes (or other token of appreciation) to award to each other for doing a good job.

Spontaneous recognition. At Nationwide, no review process is needed to give small awards to an employee for helping a coworker or assisting a customer "above and beyond." Spontaneous recognition awards vary from region to region and offer everything from simple thank-you notes to free parking for a month.

Informal awards: Federal Express. Federal Express managers have small budgets for day-to-day spontaneous reward and recognition of employee efforts through coupons for free sodas and chocolates. Some employees find the unexpected awards, presented in front of coworkers, more meaningful than a formal reward and recognition.

Best Practices | for Reward and Recognition

Other ideas from Federal Express include putting names of top-performing customer representatives in a hat for a drawing once a month. The winner gets to work his or her "dream shift" for a week. FedEx also gives employees a "stress relief pack" consisting of silly items like Groucho Marx–style glasses, a fake nose, and a bottle of soap bubbles.

Blue ribbon service. At Katy Medical Center in Katy, Texas, employees, patients, and visitors can nominate workers for a blue ribbon by filling out a card that describes what they did to deserve the award. Employees wear the blue ribbon on their clothing. For subsequent awards, they receive gold stars, or "twinkles," to attach to the ribbon. Five twinkles earn a permanent gold star, and five permanent stars earn the employee a gold pin.

There's also an employee-of-the-month award. Workers who've received stars are eligible as well as workers recommended by their supervisors. The award is a $25 gift certificate, a brass paperweight, and free parking for a month. One of these employees is eventually selected as employee of the year and receives a $100 gift certificate and trophy.

Zero defects. Gwinnett County (Georgia) instituted two award programs that helped to improve the efficiency and quality of workers at the auto tag offices. The county gave a "zero defects award" to employees who during the course of a day made no errors in entering customer information. The prize: a Zero candy bar. The "What a Difference a Day Makes" board showed the number of people each clerk assisted. Efficiency soared as employees competed to serve the most citizens while maintaining the highest accuracy.

Best Practices | for Reward and Recognition

Plus people recognition program. North Carolina Memorial Hospital in Chapel Hill, North Carolina, rewards employee efforts to improve patient service. Each quarter, 12 people are selected through peer and supervisor recommendations. Winners receive certificates and pins plus recognition through internal publicity and a celebration party in their department. At the end of the year, all 48 winners enjoy an evening at a dinner theater.

Selection teams. Hampton, New York–based Omni Hotels has selection teams comprised of employees who select award recipients. Criteria for an award nomination include such things as making decisions outside one's area of job responsibility, promoting the hotel on one's own initiative, performing a heroic deed, working extended hours or working on a day off, and so on.

A single rose. At one USAA location, managers reward service employees who receive compliments by presenting them a single rose in view of all the other employees. They also hand out ribbons, give verbal praise, read customer letters at staff meetings, and reprint the letters in the employee newsletter.

Pat on the back. Basic American Foods uses a variation of the Pat-on-the-Back form to recognize employees. When someone sees someone else doing something commendable, he or she fills out a form (printed on pads of yellow stickies and placed near the employee cafeteria) and places it on a special Pat-on-the-Back bulletin board for all to see.

Reward on the spot! At USG, people who do something innovative are presented a $50 check in front of their peers.

Best Practices | for Reward and Recognition

Spotlight employees. Liberty Corporation publishes a customer service newsletter on its intranet. *The Competitive Edge* gives tips and features a column, "The Liberty Spotlight," which focuses on new and special ideas and includes a picture of the person in the spotlight. The story is also posted on three bulletin boards in the complex.

Spirit award. Hill Air Force Base in Utah uses a peer-rating system that crosses organizational lines to nominate employees who have done an outstanding job. The nomination then passes through supervisory chains. Nominees who are approved receive a jacket with the base's logo and "Spirit of Hill AFB" on it.

Offer cash rewards on an ongoing basis. For someone getting entry-level wages, even small cash rewards can be important.

Award personal days for special achievements. Some workers may value and appreciate time off as much as cash.

Prescription | for Action

- Identify and reward top performers and publicly recognize their accomplishments.
- Ensure that managers and supervisors also receive recognition.
- Reward managers, teams, and employees that improve the organization's productivity.
- Allow your workers the ability to reward each other's performance. Peer pressure is a terrific tool to create the behavior you need for success.
- Allow employees to design the reward and recognition program.
- Consider the impact of both intrinsic and extrinsic awards.
- Ensure that all your managers are able to show appreciation to their workforce.

Chapter | Ten

Help People Move Up or They Will Move Out

Allowing people to reach their potential, to become all they are capable of becoming, is not just a manager's greatest challenge but also has the most impact on retention. When people can grow, they will stay. Through job titles, training and development, team assignments, and new opportunities, a company can set into place a program that encourages employees to make the most of their talents.

Akio Morita, in his book about Sony, called the American human resources (HR) management system obsolete. He compared the American process of creating a job description and hiring a person to fill the job to building a brick wall. People become like bricks, filling narrow job descriptions and being squeezed into a wall with other bricks. Sony practices a more holistic approach: it hires a person and designs a job that takes advantage of the individual's unique talents and abilities.

Make no mistake about it: all organizations will do a better retention job by spending more resources on training and development. Giving people the freedom to create, learn, and grow is a powerful force in a good retentionship strategy. A business that provides education and training will be more competitive and productive and will win the loyalty of its workforce.

Training and development make sense for two main reasons: (1) they are good for the individual and (2) they are good for the organization.

Good for the Individual, Good for the Organization

Training, education, and degree completion programs have become one of the most desired employee benefits available. Among younger job seekers, the opportunity to learn new skills is the number one benefit.

Gen X and Gen Y workforces view training and development as critical. They value the opportunity to advance and make more money. They also want to make a bigger contribution and have a marked fear of failing or falling behind in a competitive world.

Satisfying these desires with training accomplishes personal and organizational goals. Well-trained employees are more capable and willing to assume more control over their jobs. They need less supervision, which frees management for other tasks. Employees are more capable in answering customer questions, which builds better customer loyalty. Employees who understand the business complain less, are more satisfied, and are more motivated. All of these lead to better management-employee relationships.

An American Management Association (AMA) survey of 352 HR executives also confirmed that skill enhancement issues were of top importance to employees. "Investing in employees' future is more important than immediate compensation," said Eric Rolfe Greenberg, AMA's director of management studies. "Programs that improve work skills and future career development are seen as particularly effective."

The AMA survey identified the following skill enhancement techniques and the percentage of companies employing them as a retention strategy:

Skill Enhancement Issue	% of Organizations
External conferences/seminars	78.1%
Tuition reimbursement	67.3
Managerial training	66.8
Company support for degree	62.2
Interpersonal skills training	56.8
Technical training	54.5
Employability training	35.2

Companies and managers that care about employee development make a lasting impression and earn lasting loyalty. Years ago when I was in the military, I took the time to coach one of my soldiers on getting a college education. We would sit down regularly to discuss his plans for the future. When we were transferred to different organizations, we lost track of each other until years later, when Sergeant White called me.

Sergeant White had taken my advice and gone to college. Now the army was promoting him; my interest in his future had made such an impact on him that he wanted me to come to Ft. Bragg, North Carolina, to pin on his new rank. This was a great honor. I've never forgotten what he told me: "Sir, you were the only officer who took the time to help. I can't tell you how much that meant to me."

The Bottom Line: Profitability and Productivity

Businesses need skilled workers, and a good training and development program attracts them—and also boosts productivity and profitability. A report from the American Society for Training and Development (ASTD) showed that a gap is emerging between companies that invest heavily in training and those that spend less and that the gap may trigger bottom-line repercussions. Companies that continue to increase spending on training are more likely to meet the technological requirements of their business. "A company can invest all the money it wants in technology, but if there is no one around who knows how to run the machines, fix the machines, or to figure out how the machines fit in with the overall business goals, a company may never bridge the chasm," said Laurie Bassi, ASTD vice president of research.

A preference for investing in machinery over people is hobbling many manufacturing plants, says Marty Cohen, vice president of client services and programs at the Work in America Institute, Scarsdale, New York. "There certainly is more than one generation of managers brought up in the command-and-control system who don't feel comfortable managing empowered employees." But plants that are considered world class and achieve the best rates of performance are not reluctant to empower and train workers.

In a study of more than 3,100 U.S. workplaces, the National Center on the Educational Quality of the Workforce (EQW) found that on average, a 10.0 percent increase in a workforce's education level led to an 8.6 percent gain in total productivity. But a 10.0 percent increase in the value of equipment increased productivity just 3.4 percent.

The ASTD study showed that leading-edge companies trained 86 percent of employees whereas average companies trained only 74 percent. Leading-edge companies also spent twice as much per employee. Companies that invest the most in workplace learning, the study showed, yielded higher net sales per employee, higher gross profits per employee, and a higher ratio in market-to-book value.

Why Doesn't Every Company Train?

Statistics like these from the ASTD study make it hard to believe that there are still companies out there that ignore training. But it's true. Some companies perceive training as expensive. "I can't afford to train my employees," they say. "We just want them to perform minimally and acceptably." Worse, they may be reluctant to invest in training because they believe employees with more skills will demand more money. "I'll keep them ignorant and not pay them more" pretty much sums up this attitude.

These companies are ignoring the fact that the more they invest in their people, the more productivity they get. This is especially true for companies in low-wage, high-turnover industries whose entry-level workers may lack basic job and life skills. But all companies that are serious about productivity and retention should plow a significant amount of profits back into employee training and development.

Overseas companies tend not to skimp on training. A friend of mine recently visited a manufacturing plant in Monterrey, Mexico, that places great importance on education and development. Of the 80 or so people on salary, half of them have a master's degree. Many have attended major universities in the United States. The plant manager is so serious about education that if the plant won't subsidize tuition, he offers a personal subsidy. Little wonder the plant is so productive and its employees so loyal.

Create a Career Ladder

Now that neither advancement nor lifetime employment is a given, companies need to help employees create their own career ladder.

Use the Individual Retention Profile introduced in Chapter 11 to help pinpoint the kind of skills a particular employee would benefit from developing. Sit down with the employee and present a menu of training choices. Tell the person that even though your company may not be able to guarantee promotions or pay raises, you still want to give the person an opportunity to acquire new skills. Talk about the person's career path. Explain what you need the person to accomplish, and ask about his or her hopes and dreams. Together, you can develop a training program customized for the individual and his or her

skills, position, and ambition. Development for managers may
focus on delegating, counseling, coaching, handling difficult
employees, or refining soft skills. Technical people will appreciate training in new applications and techniques.

Outlining a formal developmental program will give the
person a sense of direction as well as a feeling of career
progress even without a raise. That sense of progress is important. No employees, as Chapter 3 made clear, want to feel as
though they are working only for a paycheck. And everyone
will feel proud knowing the company wants to invest in them.

Continual learning is a must for IT personnel, for whom
education and training are prerequisites for employment.
Because they know their skills can get stale quickly, they insist
on continual training. For these workers, an individual comprehensive training and development plan must include
plenty of just-in-time and on-the-job training.

Training Programs That Work:
Bay Networks and Dell Computer

When former Intel executive David House became CEO of Bay
Networks, he realized the troubled computer manufacturer's
problems would require creating a new culture. "Culture is
what people fall back on when there are no instructions,"
House explained. "It gives you rules for when there are no
rules and it provides a common language for moving forward."

House created four courses to teach the practices that he
had set in place at Intel: decision making, straight talk, managing for results, and effective meetings. He taught the courses
to Bay's 120 highest-ranking executives who, in turn, taught
the same courses to the other 6,000 employees.

Despite chaos for a couple of weeks, House's teachings
instantly hit home and produced results. Bay reversed a
$285 million loss in fiscal 1997 with $89 million in profits the
first six months of fiscal 1998. Final proof was Bay's sale for $9
billion in 1999 to Canadian telecommunications giant Nortel.

Dell Computer Corporation also has innovative work practices. Every Dell employee's job responsibility includes finding and developing a successor—not just when he or she is ready to move into a new role but as an ongoing part of the performance plan.

In addition, when Dell promotes employees, they are given fewer responsibilities, not more. "When a business is growing quickly, many jobs grow laterally in responsibility, becoming too big and complex for even the most ambitious, hardest-working person to handle without sacrificing personal career development or becoming burned out," Chairman and CEO Michael Dell wrote in his book, *Direct from Dell: Strategies That Revolutionized an Industry.*

How to Show Your Commitment to Training

- Begin the process of becoming an employer of choice in your industry. Gather information on what is needed and sell it to top management.
- Give bonuses to those who take the time to improve themselves.
- Have a tuition assistance program available for all employees.
- Make sure the CEO and other top managers show support by attending various training programs.
- Ensure managers teach classes to other workers.
- Measure how many hours each employee spends in training each year.
- Provide just-in-time training to employees. If they know they will immediately be able to use new skills, they'll be more motivated to learn.
- Each meeting should begin with the question, "What new things have we learned recently?"
- Focus on improving individuals' weaknesses and their strengths as well.
- Identify organizational core competencies and provide necessary training.
- Allow younger members of the workforce to train older employees.
- Eliminate training programs that are obsolete or no longer needed.
- Have the training department identify new training requirements.

Using Education to Attract and Keep a Part-Time Workforce: United Parcel Service (UPS)

Education is a major benefit for a college-age workforce. That's why UPS created the Earn and Learn Program, which allows UPS to recruit and retain valuable employees—a critical task for a company that serves more than 200 countries and territories and employs more than 330,000 people.

UPS's Earn and Learn Program, available in 40 locations, offers part-time employees up to $23,000 in educational assistance. More than 10,000 employees have enrolled in the program nationwide. As of September 1999, UPS had paid out over $9 million in tuition assistance.

Part-time UPS employees are eligible for Earn and Learn the day they are hired and qualify for $3,000 in education assistance per calendar year with a lifetime maximum of $15,000. For part-time management employees, the benefits are increased to $4,000 per calendar year with a lifetime maximum of $20,000. Part-time jobs at UPS are ideal for students attending college. All employees typically earn a starting salary of $8.50 to $9.50 an hour, receive full health benefits, a 401(k) plan, paid vacations, and weekends off.

In addition to UPS's Earn and Learn education assistance, both management and nonmanagement employees at UPS are eligible for student loans administered by ConSern, an educational loan organization. Employees at the approved locations are eligible for loans of $2,000 per calendar year with an $8,000 lifetime maximum. Depending on how long a student is employed, UPS will pay off the loans in cumulative amounts. Program benefits also cover approved mandatory fees and the cost of books and software up to $65 per class.

Years Employed	Percentage Paid
One	50%
Two	75
Three	100 (up to $6,000)
Four	100 (up to $8,000)

Earn and Learn is available to student employees at any time during the year. If a student decides to sign up midsemester, benefits will be prorated accordingly. In addition, students in the Earn and Learn Program may enroll at the college or university of their choice. However, by enrolling at a partnering school, tuition, approved mandatory fees, and up to $65 in books per class will be paid by UPS with no up-front cost to the student. Currently, 72 schools have partnered with UPS to provide this deferred billing option. Students who enroll at a nonpartnering school must pay costs in full and will be reimbursed after they complete their courses with a passing grade.

Janie Barnett, president of the National Student Employment Association calls UPS's Earn and Learn Program "the most comprehensive education assistance package of its kind." Since starting the program, UPS has improved retention rates among enrolled employees by 30 percent.

Using Mentoring to Broaden Horizons

Mentoring was the management buzzword of the 1990s. Find a mentor and find success, people were told.

Mentoring remains an effective tool for personal development, but the rules are changing. The old rules that governed traditional mentor relationships have been replaced by a new set.

To cultivate effective mentor relationships in your workplace, strive to do the following:

- Look for mismatches. Don't pair people with folks who are alike, but rather pair people who will challenge each other.

- Seek mentors at all levels. In the old paradigm, a mentor was someone higher up the ladder than the "mentee." Encourage people to seek out mentors and teachers with parallel responsibilities or, when it comes to technology, younger people whose technological skills far exceed their lower rank. Sometimes the people who have the best solutions to problems are the people facing those problems themselves.

- Mix and match. One-on-one relationships are passé. No one person has all the answers or can be responsible for another's success. Carol Bartz, CEO and chairman of Autodesk, Inc., in San Rafael, California, recommends creating a "personal mosaic" of several experts rather than depending on one individual. Create a group of experts you can consult for specific needs and issues. If you need assistance with management—go to Mary. If you need help with change, see José, and so on. This approach also softens the impact when a mentor leaves the company.

- Have protégés pick their mentors. Once, mentors selected the people they wanted to groom. Now the power is shifting. At Apple Computer, a group of employees started a formal mentoring program that taught people whom to recruit as their mentors. Just a few weeks later, all participants had mentors, and a few months later, a third had been promoted.

- Everyone needs mentors. Mentoring is no longer just for the young. At Procter & Gamble, a reverse mentoring program tutors senior executives about issues facing women. "What you need is a mindset that allows you to learn from those around you, no matter who they are," says Jean Otte, founder and CEO of Women Unlimited, a New York–based career development company.

How to Develop the Potential of Your Workforce

- Explain the big picture for the company and how this influences their employment and growth.
- Provide feedback on each employee's performance. Be specific; mention a particular situation or activity.
- Make sure employees understand the company's expectations.
- Involve employees in the decision-making process whenever possible.

- Listen to their ideas and suggestions.
- Give them room to do the job without unnecessary restrictions.
- Pay for employees to attend workshops and seminars.
- Offer on-site classes where employees can learn new skills or improve old ones.
- Challenge employees with lots of responsibility.
- Assign them a coach or mentor to help them with development.

Psychological Payment: Job Titles Reflect Company Attitudes

The right job titles provide status and self-esteem and can help you reduce turnover. People care about their job titles. Sometimes they will even choose the better title over more pay. A recent graduate with a desire to move up in a chosen career field may feel that acquiring a title that will look good on a résumé is worth accepting a little less money. Recruiters have discovered that they receive a better response with well-chosen job titles. Sales associate is boring, bureaucratic, and easy to skip over in the classifieds. Chief of client relations will attract much more attention!

The president of a computer service company once tried an experiment: he offered new hires at a distant location a choice between the title of sales manager and salesperson. Although the salesperson position paid $2,000 a year more, most people took the manager title.

When a bike store owner asked me what he could do to keep one of his employees from quitting, I said, "Ask him what job title he would like." It turned out he wanted to be called the director of bike operations (DBO). The job title changed his attitude about his job and sounded impressive to his friends, too.

Director of bike operations has terrific ego appeal. And that's fine. People want to be proud of their job titles. We have to get over the bureaucratic concept that only certain people

get certain job titles and business cards. Allow a little freedom
of choice, and you'll reap plenty in loyalty.

The ultimate goal is to energize people and make them feel
good about their job. If it's a choice between losing a good
employee and a job title—I'd go with the job title anytime and
especially because giving an employee a prestigious title is one
way to recognize and reward when a raise is not affordable.
Here are a few examples to consider:

Senior vice president of great people   Chief talent scout
Director of fun & games   Culture czar
Sultan of sound bites   Director of consumer delight
Top dog   Digital yenta
Prince of pine   Chief acceleration officer
Person in charge   Employee #1
Culture team leader   Director, mind and mood

Best Practices | for Helping Employees Move Up

"Keep your promise" list. Employees often gripe that companies don't keep their promises. For example, who has been promised a promotion, education, and a new assignment? Keep a list of these promises and make sure they are fulfilled or the person is kept posted on their status.

Prevent plateaued employees. One reason employees leave a company is because they reach a plateau and begin looking for new challenges. AT&T retains such employees with a program called Resource Link. Designed to function as an in-house temporary service, Resource Link lets employees with diverse management, technical, or professional skills "sell" their abilities to different departments for short-term assignments.

Value the experience of middle managers. Unlike the United States, where companies sometimes consider middle management dead weight, Japanese companies depend on middle managers to push everyone on the team to a higher level of shared understanding. A group's knowledge base can become a major competitive advantage.

Invent a new job. A 12-year veteran at Charles Schwab was considering leaving the company—until his boss allowed him to invent a new job as organizational troubleshooter that drew on his technical and business skills. Now vice president in Schwab's Electronic Brokerage group, he acknowledges that creating his own job let him "change things and get charged up about work again," calling it "the key to my staying."

Best Practices | for Helping Employees Move Up

Encourage hallway training. A study to see how much information coworkers shared informally demonstrated that during a typical week at one company, over 70 percent of the 1.000 workers in the study shared information with fellow employees. Fifty-five percent asked coworkers for advice. This spontaneous exchange took place during the following: meetings; exchanges with customers, supervisors, and mentors; on-the-job training; site visits; cross-training; shift changes; same-level employee communication; and simply doing one's job. The next time you see employees talking during shift changes, in the halls, or at coffee breaks, remember that you may be witnessing learning in progress.

Use "stand-ups" to reinforce company culture. The Ritz-Carlton Hotels have always made training and development a top priority. Today Ritz-Carlton practices something called "stand-ups" before each shift. All employees across the globe receive a 10- to 15-minute class on the same topic. The shift leader inspects each employee for the proper uniform, nametag, and appearance. The stand-up may also include questions about one of Ritz-Carlton's 20 customer service principles. The stand-up concludes with announcements and a discussion of guest preferences, and then everyone is ready to begin the shift.

Brown-bag luncheon. An office at the Federal Energy Regulatory Commission uses brown-bag luncheons as training initiatives.

Best Practices | for Helping Employees Move Up

Chick-fil-A University. Chick-fil-A is a popular restaurant chain. Its retention rates are some of the lowest in the industry as the result of its commitment to training. Through its Chick-fil-A University, new store owners (called operators) benefit from a comprehensive seven-week training program. Classes for three weeks are held in a classroom in Atlanta; two weeks of training take place in the field. After a one-week reinforcement phase, operators spend five days at their restaurant working with a coach from corporate headquarters who helps them solve problems and review everything they learned during the seven-week process.

New Restaurant Opening Team. Before Friendly's Ice Cream Corporation opens a new restaurant, it sends in its New Restaurant Opening Team. This team of certified trainers from other Friendly restaurants and its leader, the Top Gun, arrive two weeks before the opening to train employees, conduct rehearsals, and assist management and staff until opening day.

Prescription | for Action

- Monitor career development programs to ensure that the people chosen for training, conferences, and special projects fairly represent the workforce as a whole.

- Build accountability for retaining and developing a diverse workforce into the performance management systems for supervisors and managers.

- Hold training departments responsible for results, not just for the fun to do programs.

- Evaluate training based on trainee reaction, behavior change, and job performance improvement.

- Hire from within.

- Post career advancement opportunities.

- Establish each employee's career advancement expectations with an individual retention profile.

- Cross-train employees so people understand others' roles and responsibilities.

- Ensure that senior executives teach some courses provided to line employees.

- Perform a needs analysis to determine training needs for all employees.

- Deliver training in a just-in-time manner and provide follow-up activities to learn if skills are being used.

Chapter | Eleven

Implementing the High-Retention Workplace

W hen added to a company's culture, the eight elements of retentionship discussed in the preceding chapters can have a profound effect on the work environment that in turn will profoundly affect retention and productivity.

But even in a high-retention culture with good bosses, good people leave. Instituting a formal retentionship program has two objectives: First, it can help focus on and prevent the issues that cause people to leave, and second, it can transform people into more productive employees.

There are six major steps to the retentionship process:

1. Hold people accountable.
2. Assess the organization.
3. Measure what is important.
4. Increase employee ownership and involvement.
5. Build relationships and create a positive first impression.
6. Devise intervention strategies.

Let's look at these steps one at a time.

Step 1: Hold People Accountable

I learn a lot about businesses while sitting and listening in waiting areas. Just a few minutes is enough to tell me how an organization thinks and performs. Recently, I was sitting in the waiting area for an appointment with a senior vice president, whose department had lost several key employees, and I was there to help find solutions. I listened to the receptionist answer phone calls and route callers to various locations in the company.

One call caught my attention. Judging from what the receptionist was saying, she must have been talking to a person who was looking for a job. The receptionist's answers were curt, and she summarily ended the conversation by saying, "Oh, I can't help you with that . . . that's HR's job—you have to talk to them."

It's not just HR's job. *Everyone* should be responsible for retention. Obviously, the person most accountable, influential, and with the authority to make a difference in retention is a person's supervisor. So first let us hold the direct supervisor or manager responsible—and reward those who do a good job with employee retention.

The first major change to be made is to shift the responsibility from HR to others in the organization. *HR should not be the sole responsible agent for finding, keeping, and motivating the workforce.* HR still plays an important role, however, and remains accountable.

HR must be held responsible for ensuring that managers have the tools and training they need to do their job. HR should set up retention training programs for managers and supervisors and institute policies and procedures that create a work environment for maximum productivity.

Too often, rules limit high performance. It is important to consider the entire concept of *employment.* We unintentionally create turfdoms and psychological limitations by categorizing people as part-time, contractors, full-time, temps, white-collar, and blue-collar—all categories that limit people's potential. Sometimes these labels create a stigma. A valued employee who works part-time is better than no employee at all. Don't let antiquated rules and policies limit performance and productivity. Get rid of the "this is the way we've always done it" mentality!

According to Professor John Sullivan of San Francisco State University, most HR departments are designed for the Homer Simpsons of the world. They support and reward average performance. HR must restructure itself for the new workforce and focus on pay-for-performance plans and incentives that encourage people and managers to perform at their maximum performance level. As Chapter 2 pointed out, retentionship and productivity go hand in hand. Policies that encourage retention also promote productivity.

To facilitate accountability, consider appointing a Retention Czar to give full-time attention to all retention efforts companywide. Especially beneficial to large organizations, this kind of full-time attention can be helpful as long as it doesn't shift the responsibility away from those who have the greatest impact on the life and productivity of the employees.

Step 2: Assess the Organization

Two kinds of assessments can help pinpoint potential retention problems: (1) a regular, informal assessment of employees by their managers; and (2) a formal, twice-yearly written assessment that lets employees express their feelings about the company.

Managers, as part of a monthly staff meeting, may conduct the informal assessment. During the meeting, managers need to identify individuals whose departure would leave the company vulnerable. Who would be the hardest to replace? Who has the most key knowledge/intellectual capital? Are there certain groups of people who feel left out and disadvantaged? Who are the informal leaders in the group?

Periodically, visit job-posting Web sites and review the résumés of your key people. Or hire an outside firm to audit your organization and pinpoint issues and problem areas that may cause your workforce to pack up and head south.

Next, focus on individuals going through some form of life change—marriage, pregnancy, divorce, a child's graduation, or another important event—that could influence job satisfaction and/or may persuade or force employees to leave the organization. Life changes include:

- Friends leave the company
- Marriage, pregnancy, birth of a child
- Death of a parent
- Son or daughter graduates from college or high school
- Midlife changes
- Divorce
- Ending of major projects
- Loss of a key manager or team member
- Rumors of a takeover
- Coworker gets a promotion or pay raise

Managers and supervisors should know their employees well enough to recognize when one of these events is taking place and to consider how to address it. Not every employee's departure can be prevented. My cousin's wife recently announced her pregnancy, but my cousin is a manager at a small firm that offers no family insurance benefits. There's no question my cousin is history unless his employer is willing to change company policy.

A formal, written, internal climate assessment can help your company keep its finger on the pulse of its people's feelings about the organization. It is a particularly effective strategy for large organizations scattered in remote locations. It is a common tool among leading high-tech companies like Gateway, Inc., computer maker, which assesses one-twelfth of its employees each month.

An internal climate assessment can vary in length, but the best ones have anywhere from 50 to 200 questions that probe employees' attitudes toward the company. The questions are further subdivided into categories such as:

- Mission, vision, and values
- Change
- Diversity
- Individual competencies
- Training and development
- Compensation/promotions and benefits
- Performance evaluation
- Supervision
- Morale
- Customer service
- Communications
- Decision making
- Teamwork
- Leadership
- Organizational structure
- Technology

This kind of internal climate assessment requires foresight and forethought. First, you must come to grips with what you want to know and be willing to make changes based on the results. And you must share the results with all employees. The worst thing is hiding the results of the survey from the people who took it. The disaster of the *Titanic* may pale in comparison to what this mistake will cause. Basically, you are saying, "Our company is so bad that we are hiding the fact!"

Keep in mind that, the first time you conduct an internal climate assessment, the results tend to show more negativity. Employees use the first one to get your attention. Take the first one with a grain of salt and expect more accurate results when you repeat the assessment six to eight months later.

Step 3: Measure What Is Important

The old saying is true: what gets measured gets done. Measurement can quickly identify and pinpoint possible causes and sources of turnover. Here is a list of things to measure:

- Internal customer satisfaction scores
- Dollar amount of bonuses paid out
- Number of vacancies by department
- Number of qualified applicants who exceed job qualifications
- Number of people who quit before their first 90 days
- Department that has highest turnover and why
- Time it takes to fill vacancies
- Starting salary of new hires compared with the industry average
- Number of people promoted from within
- Applications and interviews pending
- Amount of resources (money and time) company spends on recruiting job applicants
- Department that has lowest turnover and why
- Number of job offers accepted
- Number of candidates lost to competition

The numbers can be revealing. I worked with a company that took so long to process applications and set up interviews that most applicants eventually gave up and looked elsewhere for work. But management was oblivious until I showed them the measurements.

Not all measurements will be so dramatic. A major portion of a good retentionship program is spent in making small course corrections. There's no need to oversteer the ship—especially if you discover that small adjustments to what you are presently doing are all that is required.

Step 4: Build a Sense of Employee Ownership

Employees need to feel a sense of ownership, a stake in their company and its policies. In a high-retention organization, employees have strong feelings that their contributions have a direct impact on the performance of the organization and that they can somehow share in its rewards. They know that their ideas and knowledge have some importance and impact on the operation of the organization.

One way to build ownership is to include employees in crafting policies that address retention. Guardian Industries, an 800-person glass plant in Indiana, decided to listen to its employees when it wanted to find a better way of deciding how to staff shifts. The employees decided that instead of working rotating shifts between day and evening, they would rather work permanent 12-hour shifts. The result: turnover fell by 50 percent and productivity improved accordingly. You can bet that workers' sense of ownership over the shift policy was a large factor in achieving those improvements.

Top Ten Reasons You Made a Mistake Working at this Company
When on your first day at work:

1. You had to park your car a mile away because you didn't get your parking pass in the mail.
2. You watched 18 videos on what it means to work here.
3. You read a 300-page employee handbook and signed your name saying you understood what it means.
4. Your new cubicle is being used as the coffee break area.
5. You sat in the hallway for an hour waiting for the benefits clerk to return from a long lunch.
6. You signed two dozen forms asking for information you didn't bring with you.
7. You went to meet your boss to find out about your assignments, only to find she was on vacation until next week.

8. On your invitation to the new employee reception, your name was spelled wrong.
9. Right before you went home, you got a call saying you needed to provide a specimen for the company urinalysis program.
10. That night when you were at home the senior vice president called to welcome you to the company and then said your department was being eliminated.

Step 5: Build Relationships and Create a Good First Impression

Retentionship begins on a new person's very first day on the job. Many employees decide to quit during the first two days at work. Sure, the scenario in the Top Ten Reasons box is exaggerated, but the first week at work should remain in the memory of the new hire as a positive event—a celebration that makes him or her proud to have chosen this organization.

In one organization plagued with high turnover, many employees quit during their first week of employment. Everyone just scratched their heads and hid behind the excuse, "Kids today just don't have any work ethic." Not until we sat down and started asking "why" did the real problem emerge: not the work ethic of new employees but their activities during their first week on the job. New hires were ushered into a conference room the first week to watch about 20 videos by themselves. The information was very technical and foreign to many of the employees who took jobs there. They didn't get to meet any other employees. No one took them out to lunch. No wonder, at the end of the week, they opted not to return! It is important to build relationships with coworkers during the first week of work.

Steps can be taken to ensure that the first few days at work are successful and eliminate resignations caused by unintentionally thoughtless behavior.

Before an employee's first day of work, make sure to do the following:

- Appoint a person or have a concierge call before the new hire starts work.
- Have the new hire fill out forms on the company intranet if available.
- Send a form of greeting such as a card, welcome basket, or other gesture.
- Have an HR rep call and answer questions about benefits and the like.
- Ensure that new hires know how to and where to park their cars, if applicable.

During an employee's first two days at work, make sure to do the following:

- Have a group of key employees sit down with the new person to discuss what it is like to work there. Everyone benefits: the new hire gets a support network, and key employees build their leadership skills.
- Take a digital photo of the new person and create a flyer to hang on the wall detailing about his or her hobbies, experiences, and background information.
- Introduce the new hire to the CEO/president.
- Provide a "new employee" reserved parking spot.
- Provide a copy of the organizational values, mission, and vision statement.
- Make sure the employee has a phone and e-mail directory of everyone in the organization.
- Assign an employee who enjoys working with people as a buddy to the new hire. This person is responsible for helping the new hire settle in and get acquainted with the office.

- Ensure the new hire's work area is properly equipped, loaded, and stocked ready for the first week's worth of work.

- Have a company T-shirt and/or company mug ready for the person.

- Have business cards ready.

- Take the new person out to lunch to meet the team.

- Hang a welcome sign signed by the team.

- Put pictures of new hires in the local newspaper and company newsletter welcoming them to the team.

- Send the spouse and family members some sort of welcome gift or appreciation basket.

- Have a spouse's support group invite the person's spouse out for coffee.

- Have a new employee lunch for spouses during the first month.

- Minimize the forms to be completed and signed and the videos to be viewed until later on.

- Take a team photograph.

During a new hire's first week at work, do the following:

- Fill out an Individual Retention Profile on each person. A sample IRP is included in Appendix B.

- Do a DISC profile on each person so you learn his or her motivators and communication style.

- Have someone meet the new hire after the first week and find out what went right and what went wrong.

- Reward people who are helpful to the new person.

- Put photos of the "go-to" people on a wall for the new person to see.

Individual Retention Profile.   In addition to the traditional employee orientation program, an Individual Retention Profile (IRP) can be used as a guide to stimulate important conversations between the manager and the employee during the first week on the job. The IRP helps focus on individual goals, career development, and opportunities the individual would like to achieve during his or her tenure. It provides a list of questions and fill-in-the-blank responses that can help managers discover important information about the new hire's personal and professional goals; plans and visions for the next three years; most and least enjoyable aspects of the new job; favorite form of recognition; and ideas for making the job more rewarding.

New Employee Orientation Checklist

Make sure your new employees have an opportunity to learn about every aspect of the organization. Look for ways to make the orientation comprehensive but not overwhelming.

Introduction to the Organization
- ✓ History of the organization
- ✓ Diversity policy
- ✓ EEO statement/policy
- ✓ Worksite mission
- ✓ Copy of employee handbook
- ✓ Completion of W-4 and state forms

Benefits, Compensation, and Incentives
- ✓ Health, life, and disability insurance
- ✓ Retirement benefits
- ✓ Pay procedures
- ✓ Performance evaluation
- ✓ Reward and recognition programs
- ✓ Ideas/suggestions program
- ✓ Education assistance
- ✓ Career development
- ✓ Health and wellness programs
- ✓ Flextime policies

Leaves of Absence
- ✓ Return to work

✓ Maternity leave

✓ Leave without pay

✓ Sick leave/PTO

✓ Military leaves

✓ Jury duty

✓ Bereavement

✓ Family and Medical Leave Act (FMLA)

Work Environment

✓ Tour of worksite and important places, restrooms, coffee/break areas, cafeteria (if any), coat and personal property areas

✓ Parking for vehicles, public transportation routes

✓ Proper dress

✓ Standards of conduct

✓ Employee grievance procedures

✓ Smoking policy

✓ Safety in the office

✓ Security

✓ Office computer system

✓ Equipment issue

✓ E-mail and printers

✓ Use of Internet

✓ Phone system

✓ Copy machines

Step 6: Devise Intervention Strategies

Don't be surprised by a departure—be prepared for it. Develop an arsenal of techniques you can use to respond effectively when you learn of a potential departure. First, institute an early-warning system. Ask employees to let you know if they hear about other employees who are thinking about quitting. Advance notice will give you an opportunity to try to prevent the departure. When you learn that an employee is considering another offer, take time to explore the reasons behind the move.

Many people who consider leaving jobs are only trying to escape the same problems that prompted them to change jobs before. If that's true, the same challenges will probably crop up again in the new position. Why not help the employee work on personal perceptions and attitudes in your workplace instead of moving to a new job?

When people seem unsuccessful, dissatisfied, complaining, or restless, find out why. Why are they really dissatisfied—is it compensation or something else? Pinpoint the source of the dissatisfaction. Ask these questions:

- What does it mean to be successful on the job? If the employee can clarify what is truly important, you may be able to find a way to help the person meet that criterion.

- Is the employee upset over a particular situation? Emotional reactions to situations encourage drastic steps, but drastic steps aren't always the best thing to do.

- Is the employee restless and bored in the job? Explore and discuss ways to increase the challenge. Can the person take on more responsibility or work in a different area as an avenue to an eventual more satisfying position?

- Is the person dissatisfied with compensation? Point out that higher pay in a new job may come at the cost of important benefits or quality of life.

- Pinpoint the source of the employee's dissatisfaction. The boss? The work environment? The work hours?

- Is the person just not finding meaning and a purpose in his or her responsibilities?

Encourage people to take time to think through a possible job change. Quitting may be a relief—and it may be the best thing for some people to do. But before they make their decision, help them be honest about their motivation and consider all aspects, both positive and negative.

Limited impact of counteroffers.   Making a counteroffer to an employee who has another job offer is not a sound idea.

People leave for reasons other than money, even if they say the reason is money; that may not, however, be the main reason. To offer such people more money to stay could only add insult to injury. Studies show 32 percent of those who accept a counteroffer leave within six months anyway. Keep in mind that productivity and morale may suffer in the process while they wait for another offer.

Another problem is that counteroffers leave a bad taste in the mouths of employees who stay, are working hard, and don't want to leave. In one organization I worked with, the buzz among loyal employees was that "all you had to do was whine a little bit and threaten to leave and you got a pay raise."

One solution to the pay raise problem came from Glenroy, a manufacturing firm in Wisconsin, which allows its employees to decide their own pay raises. All employees are placed in peer groups based on job classifications. Then it's up to the peer groups to decide and set the pay raises for each other. Michael Dean, the president of Glenroy, says in most cases the peer groups were tougher than management in deciding who gets pay raises; in fact, management had to readjust the recommendations upward.

Can I come back to work here?   No matter how good you think your company is, your employees always think they can find a better job elsewhere. "The grass is greener" mentality is alive and well in organizations across the country.

So keep the doors open for them to come back. Let them know that they are always welcome to return. Try to remove the embarrassment when they return. Don't make them feel like an outlaw or a mutineer. But do acknowledge their decision. If it were up to me, I'd throw a big party for a returning employee and let that person tell the other employees how great it is to work there.

If you have a large enough company, consider creating an employee alumni organization. Keep in contact with previous employees, send them newsletters, and keep recruiting and talking to them until they return. Who knows, they may refer others employees to you.

Make postmortem analysis part of the system. Every time an employee voluntarily leaves, you need to find out why. Rumors fly when an employee quits. Sometimes the rumors are more damaging than the actual departure. It is important to find out the real reasons behind the departure and not let rumors damage the morale and attitudes of those who stay.

Convene a panel of people, including the individual's boss and colleagues, to discover why the person left and what can be done to prevent the same problem, if there was one, from occurring again. Feedback on the real reason the person left may be painful, but it should be publicly disseminated as long as it does not violate anyone's rights.

Rehire your employees. An emphasis on hiring new people can cause older employees to feel ignored or forgotten. To combat this situation, consider reinterviewing all of your employees periodically. During the interview, review their training and development, identify new skills they've acquired, review their pay and benefits, and ask each one to complete an Individual Retention Profile.

Golden Key National Honor Society: Creating Change through an Implementation Team

The Golden Key National Honor Society is a unique organization designed to recognize the academic achievement of students in colleges and universities worldwide. The nonprofit organization has over 300 chapters nationwide as well as chapters in Australia, Canada, New Zealand, Malaysia, South Africa, and the United Kingdom.

The first 320 members were inducted from Georgia State University in 1977. James Lewis, one of the first members and the founder of the organization, presently serves as the executive director. This visionary leader has led his organization from one full-time staff person in 1977 to a present total of 60 full-time staff members and 25 volunteers located in two buildings in Atlanta with additional staff members in the United Kingdom, Canada, and Australia. Staff members, many of whom were student members of Golden Key prior to graduating from college, are passionate about Golden Key and its mission.

During the year 2000, Golden Key found itself facing the same challenges and opportunities that face large organizations. They asked me to conduct an internal climate assessment; design a reward and recognition program for staff members; and improve communication and service across their departments.

After meeting with the executive management team, we clarified the expectations and a methodology for change and improvement. A key issue identified in the internal climate assessment for this organization was to improve communication. I feel the best ideas for change and improvement must come from two directions—the top and the bottom of the organization.

The top of the organization is knowledgeable about the goals and strategic direction. The bottom of the organization is aware of the problems, obstacles, and limitations. In most cases, the bottom of the organization has some of the best ideas on how to resolve many of the problems. To tap into these ideas, we created an implementation team, a temporary structure that would provide input and advice and help drive commitment from the bottom up. (See Figure 11.1.)

The first step was to select the members for the implementation team. We looked for informal leaders who were respected by their coworkers and people from each area or department of the organization. Our major goal was to have team members who were ready, willing, and able to return to their respective areas and influence change from the bottom up.

Figure 11.1 Implementation Team

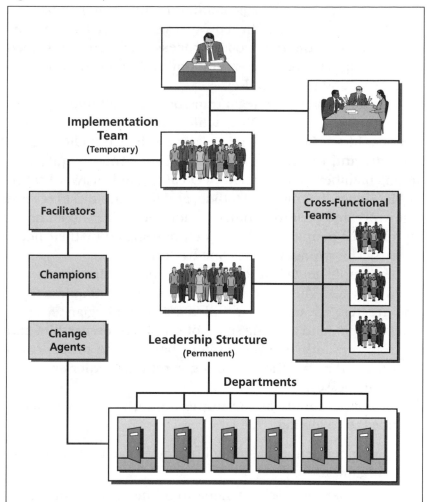

The final team included one representative from each department and one member who represented the volunteer staff. During each meeting we had at least one person teleconferenced into the meeting from another part of the United States or Canada. To allow the members to bond as a team, express their feelings, and identify issues unrestrictedly, the executive management team was excluded from the first three meetings. Then the executive director and assistant directors joined and became permanent and integral team members.

The final outcome turned out even better than we expected. During the two-month process, the members gained an even higher level of commitment and dedication both to each other and to Golden Key.

The implementation team transformed itself into a permanent committee called VOICE, which stands for Vision, Opportunities, Ideas, Communication, and Exchange. VOICE meets monthly and the role of the team leader rotates quarterly among members. Furthermore, VOICE created an award called STAR (Stellar, Teamwork, Attitude, and Recognition) to reward teamwork and positive attitudes. Each month a random drawing chooses people who have been nominated by their peers as Stars. The winner receives one day off.

The implementation team strategy has its drawbacks and its advantages. The biggest drawback is that it requires time. The greatest advantages: It builds a strong allegiance, great commitment, and a strong sense of employee ownership; and it empowers individuals to affect change. The process also eliminates the "we/they" blaming syndrome experienced in many businesses.

Other outcomes of the implementation team process include the following:

- Members gained a strong bond with each other and the organization.
- Members had more ownership of the final recommendations and were thus more likely to implement them.
- There was higher retention.
- Employees enjoyed greater satisfaction.
- Improved understanding between management and all levels was notable.
- There was improved communication throughout the organization.

This process illustrates the difference between a low-retention and high-retention workplace. Of course, people want to be paid well, but they also want input, to be involved, and to have a stake in how the organization manages itself.

Guidelines for Using an Implementation Team

- Pick people who want to be part of the process.
- Build a bond between members early on.
- Expect it to take longer than you originally estimated.
- Have a neutral individual or consultant to facilitate each meeting.
- Expect to encounter all ranges of emotions and issues.
- Require key executives to participate in the meetings.
- Rotate the role of the team leader among different people.
- Avoid distractions and consider going off-site for meetings.
- Provide recognition to team members who participate.

During an off-site retreat, the Golden Key leadership team developed a set of guiding principles to help steer its organization and keep it on course during times of change. These guiding principles are an internal document used primarily as a value statement for how the society treats its employees and carries out its work.

Golden Key National Honor Society Guiding Principles

We are committed to treating our staff with fairness and respect and understand that each employee is integral to our success.

We are committed to creating a positive, healthy work environment that promotes open communication.

We are committed to the growth, development and recognition of our staff.

We are committed to recognizing all students who meet our standards.

We are committed to a global perspective in setting and achieving our goals.

We are committed to community service.

We are committed to diversity.

We are committed to innovation and proactive change.

(Permission granted to reproduce by the Golden Key National Honor Society Executive Director.)

Hiring for Retention

You just hired a new employee. She wasn't your first choice, but because it is difficult to find good employees, you decided to lower your standards and hire her anyway. What harm can it do, you ask? The next day the scenario goes like this:

> "Welcome to your first day at work," says the store manager. "We are going to have you work as a cashier. It is very important you show up for work on time and please smile and greet each customer."
> The very next morning, the new employee arrives 15 minutes late—"car trouble." The following day, a customer complains that the new employee overcharged her $16. Lo and behold, Friday, the new employee calls in sick. After a month, her negative attitude starts affecting other employees. The new employee starts an argument with one of your best employees. Then the good employee quits and storms out the door.

Does it matter whom you hire? Is lowering your standards a good strategy? Finding the right person for the right job is critical to business success. Chances are you have made some bad hiring decisions in the past. With recruiting costs continuing to escalate, a wrong choice is going to cost you thousands of dollars. Can you afford to make a mistake?

Many people with hiring responsibilities are not aware that bad choices damage healthy organizations. Short-sighted decisions often lead to disastrous results. Never lose sight of the fact that your hiring decisions are critical to the growth, productivity, and long-term retention of your employees.

Carol Hacker, an internationally recognized consultant and trainer in the field of recruiting and retention, is author of the book *The Costs of Bad Hiring Decisions and How to Avoid Them.* Several of her ideas and concepts are reflected in this section. Before you hire or promote, keep in mind the following:

- Your best pool of candidates exists within your organization, a fact which is often overlooked; promote from within as often as possible.

- Posting job openings so current employees know what it takes to be considered is a good business decision.

- Explaining your reasons for rejecting internal candidates is more than common courtesy. It's a morale booster for those whom you may want to consider later.

- Consider the possibility of not filling a vacancy. You may want to redistribute the workload, eliminate parts of the job, or pay overtime to current employees as less expensive alternatives to hiring another person.

Interviewing is the most widely used technique to hire and promote applicants, but interviewing alone is unreliable in today's market. A more sophisticated approach is needed. One reason interviewing is unreliable is because most of today's job seekers are proficient at interviewing—they already know what they are supposed to say. They can make a good presentation and bluff their way through. Furthermore, job résumés are often exaggerated and unreliable. Traditional interviewing practices fail for several reasons:

Lack of preparation.   The first impression lasts a long time. Before the interview, make sure you understand the key elements of the job. Develop a simple outline that covers general job duties. Possibly work with the incumbent to get a better idea of what the job is about. Screen the résumés and applications to gain information for the interview. Standardize and prepare the questions you will ask each applicant.

Lack of purpose.   Not only are you trying to determine the best applicant, but you also have to convince the applicant that this is the best place for the applicant to work. Today's workers have many more choices and job opportunities to choose from.

Lack of clearly defined job competencies.   Each job can have anywhere from 6 to 14 job competencies. Identify the behaviors, knowledge, motivations, and qualities that incumbents need to be successful in the job. If the job requires special education or a license, be sure to include it on your list also. There are several assessments and profiles available to help ensure you have a good match between the applicant and the job.

Lack of structure.   The best interview is a structured process. This doesn't mean that the entire process is inflexible without spontaneity. What it means is that each applicant is asked the same questions and is rated consistently. A structured approach helps avoid bias and gives all applicants a fair chance.

Other Resources

The Costs of Bad Hiring Decisions and How to Avoid Them, by Carol Hacker
Every Employee's Guide to the Law, by Joel Lewin III
Hiring Great People, by Kevin Klinvex et al.
Keeping Your Valuable Employees, by Suzanne Dibble
Society of Human Resource Managers: <www.shrm.org >

A successful interview should determine if there is a match between the individual and the job. Furthermore, a good interview process allows you to understand an applicant's behavior, values, motivations, and qualifications. The best ways to accomplish this is by using behavioral-based questions, role plays, and situational questions. Some examples are shown below.

Behavioral questions are used to evaluate the applicant's past behavior, experience, and initiative:

- Give me an example when you . . .
- Describe an incident where you went over and beyond the call of duty.
- Tell me about the time you reached out for additional responsibility.
- Tell me about the largest project you worked on.

Situational questions evaluate the applicant's judgment, ability, and knowledge. The interviewer first gives the applicant a hypothetical situation such as this:

You are the store manager of a hardware store. One of your employees has just told you that he thinks another worker is stealing merchandise from the store.

- What should you do?
- What additional information should you obtain?
- How many options do you have?
- Should you call the police, and if so, when?

Many times in my seminars, I ask people to participate in role play scenarios. Using role play situations provides effective ways to learn and practice new skills. They can also be used during the interview process to determine the skills and personal charisma of people during stress. For example, if you are interviewing a customer service representative, you can use a role play to see how this person would manage an irate customer. When using role plays, consider the following guidelines:

- It is a good idea to write the situation down on paper. Give applicants time or a short break to "get into character" before beginning the role play.

- Give candidates clear guidelines and background information so they thoroughly understand the situation.
- Allow them to ask questions before you begin.
- Debrief applicants at the conclusion of the role play. Ask them to tell you how they thought they did and how they could have done it differently. Conclude the role play in a positive way.

Preemployment Screening and Assessments

As I noted earlier in this section, the traditional interview is never 100 percent reliable. Yes, a structured approach will improve your chances, but it is important to go one step further. Preemployment screening is an important aspect of the hiring process for a growing number of employers. A better approach is needed.

Many organizations are now turning to behavior assessments and personality trait testing for both hourly workers and managers. Back in the late 1990s, only 5 percent of Fortune 500 companies used some type of assessment. Today, that figure is climbing to 65 percent. A year 2000 study by the American Management Association showed that nearly half of 1,085 employers polled use at least one assessment in their interviewing process.

Javier Lozano, SPHR (Senior Professional in Human Resources), an organizational capability coordinator for Chevron USA, recently told *HR News:* "A validated pre-employment test can be a strong predictor of future performance and whether an applicant is a good fit for the job. If used correctly, a validated test can be one of the best retention tools available to the employer."

One bank using computerized assessments selected people who sold $60,000 more services and products annually. A manufacturing company, using the assessment, hired people who generated $21,600 more per year than the company average and $42,000 more than those who received failing scores with the assessment. By using behavioral interviewing processes and assessments, Ritz-Carlton Hotels were able to reduce their turnover from more than 100 percent to less than 30 percent.

By using various assessments and profiles, our company has been able to help clients reduce turnover and improve the quality of their workforce. Behavioral profiles and assessments have proven to be an effective tool for improving the management of an organization. They provide an accurate analysis of employees' behaviors and attitudes otherwise left to subjective judgment. I provided a more thorough discussion about the DISC behavioral profile in Chapter 3.

Assessments, Profiles, and Preemployment Resources

Organization	Phone	Web Site
Assessment Plus, Inc.	800-536-1470	<www.assessmentplus.com>
Chart Your Course International	800-821-2487	<www.ChartCourse.com>
Personal Decisions International	800-633-4410	<www.pdi-corp.com>
QWIZ, Inc.	800-367-2509	<www.qwiz.com>.
Strategic Information for Teambuilding Inc.	770-918-1039	<www.war4talent.com>

Best Practices | for Welcoming New Hires and Preventing Departures

New hire "boot camp." To train new people in the company culture as soon as possible, Prentiss Property Services puts new property managers through an intensive weeklong boot camp. Customized for managers, engineers, development officers, facilities managers, and administrative assistants, the boot camps help 12 to 16 new hires learn all aspects of their job from paperwork to customer service and technical aspects. Even though the boot camps have improved communication and employee retention, their main goal is to improve customer service. The results are paying off big time. Prentiss has won numerous awards and has been voted the best in its industry for customer service.

Buddy system. Redken has a buddy system for new presenters that represent their company. When a new person comes on board, a veteran acts as a coach to help the person through the tough and embarrassing times of becoming a strong presenter. The coach feels empowered when selected by the supervisor, and the "newbie" is assimilated more quickly into the organization and becomes a better team member.

Club 1230. The Boys and Girls Clubs of America has a unique way to improve teambuilding in its Atlanta office. Once a week, everyone gathers to meet and greet new employees and share news of the good things happening in the organization. This helps tear down functional silos, improves communication, and makes everyone feel part of the same team.

Best Practices | for Welcoming New Hires and Preventing Departures

First-Friday meeting. During its monthly First-Friday meeting, new employees at an Atlanta-based HR company stand up and talk about their decision to join the company. At the end, everyone gives the new employees a standing ovation. This technique makes the new employees feel welcome and makes the older employees feel more special about working there.

Employee scavenger hunt. Managers from the Peasant Restaurants break into teams of five to go on a scavenger hunt in the corporate offices. But instead of looking for things, managers look for people. Using a sheet of names that includes a little-known fact about each corporate office worker and his or her job responsibility and hobbies, managers must track down and get to know the employee. New managers also share information about themselves, which begins a personal relationship between the manager and employee. Employees share in the process by providing the managers with cookies and other refreshments.

"Lunch bunch." At the Boys and Girls Clubs of America, each month a different group of people is appointed the lunch bunch. The group's job is to travel around the office inviting employees—particularly new employees and people from other departments—to eat lunch with them. It's an excellent way to build loyalty and team spirit.

Prescription | for Action

- Focus on building relationships among your employees at work.
- Make employee satisfaction just as important as customer satisfaction.
- Start measuring turnover and associated costs.
- Continuously evaluate and improve processes to collect data.
- Begin retention strategies before a new employee's first day at work.
- Review your internal customer satisfaction data as often as you do financial data.
- Show how changes in employee satisfaction have an impact on financial performance.
- Do internal customer satisfaction surveys to see what managers and employees want more of and less of.
- Identify how your employment practices differ from your competition.
- Hold managers and supervisors directly accountable for retention in their respective departments.

Appendix | A

Chart Your Course Worker Retention Survey Results

The following survey was conducted during September and October 2000 by Chart Your Course International.

- Survey sent to 3,000 people with 317 respondents from national and international organizations, including 138 female respondents and 179 male respondents. Respondents represented small businesses, corporations, and government organizations.
- Percentages were rounded up or down to the nearest whole number.

1. What are the reasons you stay at your present job? (Check all that apply)

Challenging job assignments	59%	Feel appreciated for what I do	35%
Salary	55%	Career opportunities	34%
Interesting work	53%	Makes me feel good	27%
Benefits	48%	Relationships	26%
Flexibility in work hours	45%	Autonomy	25%
Good boss	41%	Have friends at work	20%
Feel like we have a purpose	39%	Like to travel	12%
Work assignments vary	38%	No time to look for new job	10%
Pride	37%	Bring pets to work	9%
Location is convenient	36%	Other	8%

Source: Survey designed and developed by Chart Your Course International, 770-860-9464. <www.ChartCourse.com>

2. How would you rate the supervisors you work for now? (Check one)

Very good	35%	Poor	10%
Average	26%	Does not apply	7%
Exceptional	21%		

3. Do you feel your company has your best interests at heart? (Circle one)

a) Most of the time   45%
b) Sometimes   39%
c) All the time   8%
d) Never   7%

4. How important is company loyalty to you? (Circle one)

a) Very important   38%
b) Highly important   30%
c) Important   27%
d) Not important   5%

5. How important is feeling appreciated for your work by your coworkers and superiors? (Circle one)

a) Very important   42%
b) Highly important   41%
c) Important   16%
d) Not important   2%

6. Are you presently considering leaving your job for another? (Circle one)

No   64%
Yes   30%
Maybe   6%

7. Was the attitude of your direct supervisor/manager the primary factory in your quitting a previous job? (Circle one)

No   61%
Yes   35%

8. To improve your workplace environment, what would you like to see your executives/supervisors/managers do? (Check all those that apply)

Better at communicating	69%	Try new things at work	36%
Set the example	46%	Listen to my ideas	30%
Be more appreciative of		Be more fun at work	26%
what I do	39%	Other reasons	17%
Don't micromanage	37%	Get a job somewhere else	7%
Show genuine concern	36%		

9. How confident are you that you can find a better job somewhere else? (Circle one)
   a) Confident   33%
   b) Very confident   30%
   c) Highly confident   22%
   d) Not confident   14%

10. What causes you the greatest dissatisfaction at work? (Check all that apply)

Lack of appreciation	33%
Too much paperwork	27%
Problems with supervisors	23%
Lack of training and development	20%
Pay and benefits	20%
Lack of opportunity	20%
Other	19%
Fairness	18%
Problems with coworkers	16%
Commute/travel to work	15%
Boring job	9%
No flextime	8%
Family issues	6%

11. What would be the greatest single thing your company
    could do to improve retention? (Check one)

Train the managers better	32%
Listen to employees more	28%
Be willing to try something new	24%
Pay more	23%
Select the managers better	22%
Set the example first	22%
Hire better people	18%
Better benefits	13%
Other	12%
Nothing	2%

12. On a scale of 1 (Lowest) to 10 (Highest), how would you
    rate the efforts of your company to retain good people?
    (Circle the number)

    Low
1	3%
2	6%
3	12%
4	11%
5	13%
6	16%
7	17%
8	11%
9	5%
10	3%

    High

Appendix B

Individual Retention Profile

I. General Information
Name:_____ Date of interview: _____

Title: _____ Date hired: _____

Department: _____

Birthday:_____ Supervisor's name: _____

II. Background Information
Home address: _____

Home phone:_____ E-mail address: _____

Family/Partner Information:

Name: Birthday(s)

_____

_____

_____

_____

Pets: _____ Hobbies: _____

Parents: (Optional) _____

Favorite book:_____ Favorite movie: _____

Other information: _____

_____

III. Goals
Past achievements:

Personal:

Source: 2001 CYC International. To order additional forms, call 800-821-2487. <www.ChartCourse.com>

Professional:

Where do you see yourself in 1/2/3/4 years from now in our company?

What type of training/development can we provide to make you a better worker?

IV. Motivators

DISC profile: D   I   S   C

Are you thinking about quitting and, if yes, why? _____

In what ways are you different from your peers?

How do you keep yourself motivated?

Why do you like working here?

Will you feel comfortable coming to me if you become dissatisfied with your job?

What two things would you change about this place?

What have been the aspects of your work you have enjoyed the most?

What have been the least enjoyable aspects of your work?

Looking back on your life, what job has been the most fulfilling and why?

What could be done to increase your feeling of appreciation in your present job?

What is your favorite form of recognition: (Pat on the back, money, time off, etc.)

V. Leadership

What can we do to help you stay here as long as possible?

What can your manager do to make your job more rewarding?

Have we provided you a clear vision of your work?
What is expected? How does your work fit into the overall scheme of things?

Do you have the proper tools, information, and support to do your job well?

Follow-up Section (What I said I will do)

Awards and Recognition Resource List

Organization/Resources/Services	Phone
Pin Gallery Over 800 stock label pin designs	800-352-9501
<www.awards.com> Client gifts, employee recognition, trade shows, pins, plaques, trophies	800-429-2737
<www.bestimpressions.com> Customizable promotional items	800-635-2378
<www.billsims.com> Self-contained safety incentive programs	800-690-1860
<www.bravanta.com> Provides gifts, baskets, and award programs	877-427-2861
<www.Cardex.com> Incentive programs and the icard, which is a prepaid debit card allowing recipients to choose their own rewards	
<www.ChartCourse.com> Consulting organization to help companies design and implement recognition/award programs	800-821-2487
<www.fici.com> Plaques, awards, gifts, and incentive items	800-886-3367
<www.Flooz.com> Purchase "flooz" dollars that function like gift certificates. Flooz dollars can be used to buy merchandise online	

<www.Kudoz.com>
Online shopping for workplace managers, providing access
to suppliers, awards/trophies, gift certificates, art/posters,
merchandise, travel incentives, business gifts, cards/greetings   800-993-6399

<www.Recognition.org>
National Association for Employee Recognition   630-369-7783

<www.RewardPlus.com>
Offers a variety of benefits that organizations can pass along to
their workers at a discount

<www.successories.com>
Various themed awards and accessories, posters, pins,
and inspirational gifts   800-535-2773

Bennett Brothers, Inc.-Awards & Incentives   312-621-1619

<www.blockbuster.com/giftcards/corpincentive>
Blockbuster Gift Cards   214-854-3609

Bulova Corporation-Watches   718-204-3331

<www.CorporateGifts.com>
Full-service corporate incentive, recognition, and gift company   800-45-gifts

<www.halo.com>
Brand merchandise   847-647-2300

<www.jostens.com/recognition>   612-838-7672

<www.landsend.com/corpsales>
Merchandise and clothing   608-935-4875

<www.omahasteaks.com/incentive>
Food   800-228-2480

<www.llbean/corporatesales>
Clothing and merchandise   800-832-1889

Bibliography

Books, Articles, and Special Reports

"AARP Survey: Companies Do Not Use Strategies That Would Better Utilize Older Workers." News release, 11 February 2000.

Allerton, Haidee E. "Working Life." *Training and Development.* October 1999, 80.

American Society of Interior Designers. "Recruiting and Retaining Qualified Employees—By Design."

Armour, Stephanie. "Management Issues, Bad Communications Hurt Production, Morale." Democrat and Chronicle, 12 October 1998.

Arora, Samir. "What's New What's Not." *Fast Company,* January 1999, 75–77.

Associated Press. "Boeing Officials Admit Need for More Employee Input." *Atlanta Journal-Constitution,* 17 December 1995.

Association for Quality and Productivity. "Formula for Success: Balance Technology and People." February 1999, 12

"Award Effectiveness Toward Personnel Goals." 79 *Workforce Online,* no. 1, January 2000, 68.

Bartz, Carol. "What's New What's Not." *Fast Company,* January 1999.

Brooks, Nancy Rivera. "BALANCING ACT, Inflexible Companies May Pay a Steep Price in Employees and Productivity," *Los Angeles Times,* 6 September 1998.

Brudney, Juliet F. "Living With Work," *Boston Globe,* 7 July 1998.

Burritt, Chris. "Software Firm's Perks Help Cut Employee Stress," *Atlanta Journal-Constitution,* 28 February 1999, F5.

Byrne, John A. "VISIONARY vs. VISIONARY," *Business Week,* 28 August 2000, 210.

Church, Elizabeth. "The Quest to Mould a Caring Corporation," *Globe and Mail,* Toronto, 11 June 1999.

Collins, James C., and Jerry I. Porras. *Built to Last, "Big Hairy Audacious Goals."* New York: HarperCollins, 1994, 91.

Colpan, Metin. "Going the Extra Mile with Customers and Employees." *Investor's Business Daily,* 11 December 1998.

Conlin, Michelle. "And Now, The Just-In-Time Employee." *Business Week*, 28 August 2000.

Cooper, Cord. "IBD's 10 Secrets to Success." *Investor's Business Daily*, 18 December 1998.

"Core Values and Beliefs." Earthlink Annual Statement 1999.

Dahle, Cheryl. "New Rules to Grow By." *Chicago Tribune*, 6 December 1999, 6.

Dalesio, Ronald R. "Best Practices: Asia vs. the World." *Chief Executive Asia*, 27 March 1999.

Dibble, Suzanne. *Keeping Your Valuable Employees*, New York: John Wiley, 1999.

Dore, Cheryl. "Room for Mom." *Human Resource Executive*, 15 March 2001, 42–47.

"Down-Home Food, Cutting-Edge Business," *Fast Company*, April 2000.

Fandray, Dayton. "A New Generation Redefines Retirement." *Workforce Online*.

Farren, Caela. "It's Not the Money That Counts!" *News and Articles about Career, Jobs, and Employment*, 10 June 2000.

Fishman, Charles. "Sanity Inc." *Fast Company*, January 1999, 85–96.

"Five Ways to Earn Workers' Loyalty," *Managers Edge*, Preview Issue, 6.

Fleckenstein, Loren. "Keep Communication Open, So Morale Stays Up." *Investor's Business Daily*, 11 May 1999.

Frankl, Viktor E. *Man's Search for Meaning*. New York: Washington Square Press, 1984.

"Getting Along"—Your Personal Guide to Building Productive Work Relationships, Dartnell Corporation, 1999.

Grede, Robert. "'Holistic' Office Layouts can Increase Efficiency and Morale." *Milwaukee Journal Sentinel*, 20 September 1999.

Gregory, Stephen. "Making Time for Family, Fun Takes, Well, Work," *Los Angeles Times*, 11 January 1999.

Hammonds, Keith H. "Balancing Work and Family," *Business Week*, 16 September 1996.

Heldrich, John J. "Americans' Attitudes about Work, Employers and the Government," *Work Trends Survey*, Winter 1999.

"In the Company of the Family." *Financial Times*, London, 11 November 1998.

"Is Employee Loyalty Extinct?" *Atlanta Small Business Monthly*, September 2000, 8.

Jacoby, Susan. "MONEY: America's love-hate relationship with the Almighty Dollar," *Modern Maturity*, July-August 2000, 35–38.

Jones, Gareth R., and Jennifer M. George. "Lessons in Trust from Monica and Linda." *Association for Quality and Participation Newsletter,* February 1999, 5.

Johnson, Roy S. *"Best Companies," Fortune,* 3 August 1998, 941–110.

Jorgensen, Karen, *Pay for Results,* Santa Monica: Merritt Publishing, 1996.

Joyce, Amy, and Ariana Eunjung Cha. "Generation Gap," *Washington Post,* 6 August 2000, H1.

Jusko, Jill. "Always Lessons to Learn," *Industry Week,* 15 February 1999.

Kaufman, Jonathan. "Share the Wealth." *Wall Street Journal,* 9 April 1998, R10.

Kelly, Patrick. "Lose the Boss." *INC Online,* December 1997, 45.

Klinvex, Kevin et al., *Hiring Great People.* New York: McGraw-Hill, 1999.

Kohn, Alfie. "Studies Find Reward Often No Motivator." *Boston Globe,* 19 January 1987.

——. "Why Incentive Plans Cannot Work." *Harvard Business Review,* September-October 1993, 54.

——. "Tarnished Trophies." *U.S. News and World Report,* October 1993, 52–59.

Koller, Michael. "New Prentiss Employees Earn Stripes in 'Boot Camp.'" *Dallas Business Journal,* 29 January–4 February 1999.

Mallory, Maria. "Job Share, It's a creative plan to keep workers who want more balanced lives," *Atlanta Journal-Constitution,* 3 September 2000, R1.

Martin, Edward. "Making Room for Babies, Families." *Business Journal,* Charlotte, NC, 19 March 1999, 27.

McArele, Sherri, and James Ramerman. "If Boss Improves, So Will the Company." *Democrat Chronicle,* 15 October 1998.

Meyer, Peter. "Can You Give Good, Inexpensive Rewards? Some Real-Life Answers." *Business Horizons,* November-December 1994, 84–85.

Morgan, David. "Latino Culture 101." *NMPRO,* April 2000.

National Institute of Business Management. "Training, Noncash Incentives Work Best to Retain Staff." Success in Recruiting and Retaining.

Nussbaum, Bruce. "Designs for the Future." *Business Week,* 28 August 2000.

Pearson, Andrall E. "What's New What's Not." *Fast Company,* January 1999.

Randstad North America. *Employee Review: Insights into Workforce Attitudes.* 2000.

Reidy, Chris. "Benefit of Convenience." *Boston Globe,* 11 March 1999, D6.

"Retention at the Front Lines in the War for Talent." *Development Dimensions International,* July 2000, issue 9.

Rioux, Shelia M., Ph.D., and Paul Bernthal, Ph.D. "Recruitment and Selection Practices." *Development Dimensions International.*

Roberts, Paul. "PeopleSoft, Access + Info = Motivation." *Fast Company.* April-May 1998, 124-28.

Salter, Chuck. *"Designed to Work." Fast Company.* April 2000, 255-66.

———. "Insanity Inc." *Fast Company.* January 1991, 101-108.

Schlender, Brenton R. "How Sony Keeps the Magic Going." *Fortune,* 24 February 1992, 75.

Shellenbarger, Sue. "Employers Are Finding It Doesn't Cost Much to Make a Staff Happy." *Wall Street Journal,* November 1997.

Sheridan, John. "From the Field, One-Day Kaizens Minimize the Pain." *Industry Week Growing Companies.*

Sixel, L. M. "Faith in the Workplace, *Houston Chronicle,* 5 July 1999, 4D.

Skapinker, Michael. "Lifted by a Change of Atmosphere." *Financial Times,* 15 October 1998.

Smith, Gregory P. *The New Leader: Bringing Creativity and Innovation to the Workplace.* Delray Beach: St. Lucie Press, 1996.

"So What are You Doing for the Next Five Years?" *Fast Company,* May 2000.

Steinhauser, Sheldon. "Beyond Age Bias: Successfully Managing An Older Workforce." American Society on Aging; <www.asaging.org>.

Stockfisch, Jerome. "The Bennie Boom," *Tampa Tribune,* September 1999, B1.

Stueck, Wendy. "Electronic Arts Builds Workplace Wonder," *Globe and Mail,* Toronto, 21 September 1998.

"Tarnished Trophies." *U.S. News and World Report,* 25 October 1993, 52.

"The Power of Pampering: Keeping Workers in the Fold." *Chicago Tribune,* 13 September 1999, section 4.

"Training, Lifestyle Benefits Boost Employee Retention." *Industry Week Daily Web site,* 10 June 1999.

Turner, Nick. "Entrepreneur Michael Dell." *Investor's Business Daily,* 1 March 1999.

Verespej, Michael A. "Managing for Creativity: At Broderbund, It's O.K. for Employees and Ideas to Fail." *Industry Week,* 17 April 1995.

Warshaw, Michael. "Have You Been House-Trained?" *Fast Company,* October 1998.

Willax, Paul A. "Fuel Employee Productivity with a Diet of Information."
    Atlanta Small Business Monthly, September 2000, 9.

Wood, Shanna. "A Report Card on 360-Degree Assessment," *HR Atlanta
    Newsletter,* October 2000, 1.

Index

Chart Your Course International

Chart Your Course International is a management development organization that shows businesses how to improve productivity and create work environments that attract, keep, and motivate their workforce. Greg Smith is the founder and president of the organization. Greg's 25 years of leadership and consulting experience have helped cast him as a leading authority on organizational design, employee retention, change management, and leadership.

Chart Your Course International impacts the bottom line by providing a full range of services, including executive keynote consulting, internal climate assessments, training programs, coaching, and learning systems.

Greg travels internationally and has spoken to organizations in Singapore, Puerto Rico, Germany, and Canada. Some of his clients include Yamaha, Turner Broadcasting, Maxell, Rollins Inc., Ace Hardware, State Farm Insurance Company, AFLAC, BioLab, PacifiCare, Matrix Resources, KMPG, Alltell Corporation, Sweetheart Cups, the U.S. Army, Advantage Rent-A-Car, the U.S. Air Force, Chicago Federal Reserve Bank, Delta Airlines, The Young Presidents Organization, Foundation Health, Wyndham Hotels, Hallmark Cards, Service Corporation International, San Antonio School System, and UNISYS.

Greg's other publications include: *Success Passport; The Human Resources Management & Development Handbook; The New Leader: Bringing Creativity and Innovation to the Workplace; How to Attract, Keep and Motivate Your Workforce;* and *TNT: Dynamic Ideas to Reward, Energize and Motivate Your Teams.*

Chart Your Course International
2814 Hwy 212, SW
Conyers, GA 30094
770-860-9464
770-760-0581 (fax)
To contact us 24 hours a day, visit our Web site:
<www.ChartCourse.com>
To place orders: 800-821-2487